ADVENTURES WITH
ALZHEIMER'S

ADVENTURES WITH
ALZHEIMER'S

ANDREA LEE

ADVENTURES WITH ALZHEIMER'S

iUniverse books may be ordered through booksellers or by contacting:

iUniverse
1663 Liberty Drive
Bloomington, IN 47403
www.iuniverse.com
1-800-Authors (1-800-288-4677)

ISBN: 978-1-5320-7403-5 (sc)
ISBN: 978-1-5320-7404-2 (e)

Library of Congress Control Number: 2019942675

Print information available on the last page.

iUniverse rev. date: 05/28/2019

To Chris, for being the love of my life. I couldn't have done this without your love and support.

To Rob, one of my dear friends and confidant, who allows me to vent when I need to and provides the emotional support I often desperately need.

To Averi, one of my best friends, who often kept me sane and allowed me to love on sweet baby Rylee!

To my mom, my inspiration for writing this book.

To Kimberlee for being there for me and distracting me by taking me on vacation!

To Carmen with Carmen's Legacy Productions for capturing such lovely moments through her beautiful photographs!

CONTENTS

ACKNOWLEDGMENTS

There are so many close friends and family members that have inspired me to write this book, it's a challenge to know where to begin. I feel it necessary to thank my five dogs, Sasha, Mia, Red, Shiner and Gracie as well as my three cats, Bonnie, Bailey and Walter since they are a constant source of love and joy in my life.

My family, Mom, Chris and Kristina have been so very supportive and loving through the Journey with Alzheimer's and being a caregiver for my mom. Without my kids, Chris and Kristina, I would have certainly lost my mind by now. They have been here to support me every step of the way and were such a big help when mom was in the hospital with her broken hip.

To my roommate, Rob, who has been very supportive since he moved in last year, I thank you. Thank you for all the late night chats about how we deal with certain situations and handle the daily obstacles when caring for someone with Alzheimer's. The emotional support Rob provides when I am down or just mentally exhausted are greatly appreciated. Thank you for taking the time to listen, proofread my manuscript and share your experiences.

To all of my friends who have pushed, encouraged and gently nudged me to write about my daily activities with my mom as well as validating my posts on Facebook: Holly Heinsohn-Kropp, Katie Murphy, Averi

Segrest, Sandy Barr, Debbie Frase, Norma Mantz, Kylie Ebersole, Marnie Bucklew, Tracy Tucker, Teri Stratman, Donna Kuchynka, Sheri Biggs, Brenda Haile, Dr. Laura Hobgood, Jeana Garcia, Mark & Glo Hagens, Gail Lupton, Cheryl Schneider, Misty Valenta, Faline Tell, Danielle Finelli, Tawnie L'Allier, Tammy Lee, Dr. Fae Guracci, Stacey Whitten, Theresa Telfer, Dandy Kloesel, Teresa Cates, Amy Whiteley, Heide and Mike Vanegas, Linda Robbins, Mike Fort, Dee Dee Ricke, Melanie Stehle, Dee Pfuhl, Nanette Hoffer, Jeannie Veit, Linda Leist my entire Color Street family and everyone else who posted to my many, many Adventures with Alzheimer's.

INTRODUCTION

Over four years ago, my mom was diagnosed with Alzheimer's disease. I instantly became a caregiver. I was a full time student at Southwestern University and doing very well, which was quite a feat for being in my late forties! I found it necessary to withdraw from the current semester to try to sort things out and decide how I was going to balance school and staying with my mom. I hired a caregiver to be with my mom while I attended classes during the day. From late afternoon until the next morning, I was with her. The last semester before graduation, I was only away from mom about 3 hours a day and after graduation, I became mom's full time caregiver. This was all very new to me!

I wanted to write about my experiences in hopes to help others that find themselves in a similar situation or position with a parent with Alzheimer's disease. This has been the most difficult endeavor I have ever embarked on, ever! I have learned to find the humor in a rather difficult situation. There is a definite learning curve when you are new to the disease and thrown into being a caregiver for your parent. Because I was in school and caring for my mom, I had no time to attend support groups and still, to this day haven't. I sometimes believe I would benefit from a support group but just have a hard time finding the time or motivation to attend.

Please know, I have been through so much the past four years with my mom. I didn't just know what to do or say, how to act or react to what she said or did when it didn't make sense. Behind this book is four years of trial and error, finding what works and what doesn't work. I hope you find value within this book and find it useful in your everyday life, whether you are a caregiver or not.

I hope you, the readers, find my adventures with my mom helpful, heartwarming and even humorous. This book isn't for the faint of heart!

CHAPTER 1

My Story, In the Beginning

"Where is Andrea?" Mom asked. She was looking right at me. That was when I knew we were dealing with something much more serious than a concussion. I am Andrea, her daughter, and she didn't recognize me. Earlier that month, was when I first realized my mom was losing her memory, it was in July of 2013. It was a series of phone calls I will never forget. I was at home studying and my mom called. She told me she had fallen at the local Tiger Tote, but she was okay and I didn't need to worry. We talked for about ten minutes and hung up. About thirty minutes later, mom called again and we had the same conversation all over. When I hung up the second time, I was a bit worried. When I saw my mom pop up on my phone for the third time, I knew something was really wrong. She started with the same line, "I took a tumble at Tiger Tote.", but this time was different. She said she was really sore and felt like she needed to be with family. I was in classes all week, so my son, Chris drove the two plus hours to pick up mom. When she arrived I could tell she wasn't herself, she looked very tired and confused. Chris and I both thought she had a concussion from her fall. She had been to the hospital after her fall and they sent her home telling her to just rest. Which was why we put off taking her to the Dr. for a few weeks. In hind sight, we should have taken her sooner, but we were new to all of this. When mom looked right at me and asked me where "Andrea" was, I knew this was more serious.

Chris and I took mom to a local Dr. and after several tests and scans, he concluded she was suffering from Alzheimer's disease. We were devastated, heartbroken and lost. We lost the matriarch of the family that day and it was up to us to help care for her. She was prescribed meds that would slow the progression of the disease but there is nothing that can fix or reverse the damage the disease had already caused. Fortunately, moms' brain did recover somewhat from the fall and she was able to recognize me again. It was a relief that she regained some cognition and memory, but that would show to be temporary as Alzheimer's is a progressive disease. The doctor called it the long goodbye and I now understand that firsthand.

As the months passed, we were able to get into a routine with a part-time caregiver staying with mom while I was in school and I stayed at home with her the rest of the time. Being a member of an animal rescue group, Georgetown Animal Outreach, I was able to take her with me to Saturday adoption events for about a year, but as her disease progressed, she didn't have the patience to stay there the entire time. As the months passed, we had to cut out that activity altogether. She would have bouts of paranoia and feel uncomfortable being away from home. That was very difficult for me because the adoption events were an outlet I deeply enjoyed. It was nice to be able to visit with friends and meet new people. Some weeks, that was one of the two days I even left the house.

You lose friends when you are a caregiver. You aren't able to go out to lunch or dinner at the drop of a hat or even help a friend in need. Most people don't understand I can't just leave when I want to or just leave mom home to go hang out. I just don't have the freedom or luxuries I once had. Rob and I have discussed this at lengths, feeling like a prisoner in your home or where you work. Rob has time away from it, I don't. Having a caregiver come in a few hours a week is very expensive and I tend to worry about mom if they send someone new. I would rather have a friend come stay with her, but then there is the guilt you feel of asking a friend to stay with your mom, knowing it is a difficult and trying situation. I have definitely found who my true friends are. The friends that call or text or email to find out how things are, how mom is or how I am, are the friends I have kept as close as I can. I try reaching out when possible, but mom can make that a bit of a challenge most of the time. People that truly care about you, are the ones that will stick around and the ones you can truly call friends.

Being a caregiver is also rewarding. Caring for a parent that needs your assistance and support does have daily challenges but it also comes with the benefit of becoming closer to your loved one, no matter their state of mind. There is no greater love than that of a parent for their child and with Alzheimer's, it has been my experience that the roles almost reverse. You become the responsible one in the relationship and feel almost parent-like to your own parent. Much like a child, your parent becomes dependent upon you for just about everything and when they can't find you they panic, much like a child would if they felt lost from their parent. You will see that is evident in some of the following conversations.

I started posting my "Daily Adventures" on Facebook and the reception was very touching. People I have known my entire life were commenting on my stories, sharing them and thanking me for sharing my daily activities with mom. I was receiving friend requests from people I didn't know that were dealing with a similar situation or knew of someone that was. People were thanking me, telling me it helped them cope with similar situations or change what they were doing to help better a situation they were in. I write, not only the conversations, but also how I deal with tough situations. Being a caregiver is tough on its own, being a caregiver for a parent is an emotional rollercoaster! My only regret is not writing down conversations sooner!

Some of my posts aren't always about mom and Alzheimer's, some are about what I do to cope and re-direct my brain and emotional state. Being a full-time caregiver can take its toll on a person. Having a hobby or outlet is very important. Mine is sewing and being creative in other ways. Having an escape is a necessity, having one you can start and stop quickly is ideal. I also like to read books, paint and watch movies with mom, which are also great escapes.

Each post is just little snippet of our day or something noteworthy to share. My days, much like other care givers, is full of repetition and questions that usually make no sense. I hope this book can help those caring for a person with Alzheimer's, know of someone caring for someone with Alzheimer's or anyone that thinks they may find themselves in a caregivers position someday.

Mom has been living with me for 4 years now and we have had a house-mate for a little over a year. He is here Friday through Sunday, leaving really early Monday morning. He is also a caregiver for an Alzheimer's patient. He and I have learned to lean on one another for support, which helps a lot! Being able to compare notes with a peer is truly a stress reliever. I also live with five rescue dogs and 3 rescue cats that are like my children. Mom is very fond of all the critters of the house, thankfully!

To complicate matters, mom fell and broke her hip in April of 2017 and was hospitalized for about a month. I stayed with mom day and night for the first week and a half, before during and after her hip replacement surgery. I had a friend care for my pets until I was able to come home, and that was really tough on everyone. While I was with mom, one of my cats that slept with mom every night became depressed and stopped eating. When I was able to come home, I noticed he was not feeling well, so I tried to get him to eat something, but he wouldn't. I got him to an emergency vet hospital, but it was too late, he was in liver failure and would be unable to recover. He passed away the next day. After saying goodbye and dealing with such a heartbreaking ordeal, I went back to the hospital to stay with mom. Being a caregiver is tough! I don't really feel I was allowed much time to grieve the loss of my sweet Jasper because Alzheimer's never takes a break! I was there several hours in the morning into the afternoon and back again in the evening. I spent the night at home to care for my pets and most of the day with mom during her physical therapy (PT). After a few weeks of PT, mom came home. She had to be in a wheelchair for a week and kept asking me why she was in a wheelchair. After that, she was confined to a walker, which became the next source of confusion for her. She still asks if it's her walker and why she needs it. If I don't tell her the Dr. said she needs it, she often will refuse to use it or put up a fight when I ask her to use it. She still has balance issues, so I feel it is very important for her to use her walker, even when she thinks she shouldn't.

April 30, 2017

The twilight zone – Alter your reality to fit into theirs.

MOM: Did we get our luggage out of the car from our trip to New Orleans?
ME: Mom, we went to the poppy festival in Georgetown, we were only there for a few hours so we didn't need luggage.

5 MINUTES LATER...

MOM: When is everyone meeting up here? Do you think they ran into traffic?
ME: Who?
MOM: The people we were traveling with to New Orleans?
ME: We didn't... yes mom, I think they hit traffic because they left later that we did.

Sometimes you have to alter your reality to fit into theirs. We never went to New Orleans or a trip needing luggage. Sometimes it can be frustrating, but I always think about what I say before I say it. This disease is no fault of hers, she didn't bring this on from anything she did or did not do in her life. Her sister died from "complications" of Alzheimer's. I have to remind myself to be patient, as if taking care of a child.

Being able to read her mood and state of mind is paramount in deciding how to respond to what she says. Sometimes I get it right and every so often I don't. A positive response from her is very dependent on how I handle her statements and questions.

In the beginning, I often felt guilty if I had to lie or play along with her stories and questions. I felt like I was deceiving her, but her reality was very different from what was true or actually happening. Sometimes you have to just go with the flow of the conversation to keep the peace.

May 1, 2017

Sometimes fantasy is better than reality, just go with it!

Mom: When are we leaving for our trip?
Me: Where are we going?
Mom: I don't remember, I just know someone is picking us up to go to the airport.
Me: Sounds like fun. Let me know when you remember where we are going.
Mom: I sure will!

LATER...

Mom: Where did Andrea go?
Me: Which one?
Mom: (Staring at me for a minute) Oh, shit, you are Andrea... I guess I was dreaming.

LATER...

Mom: That lady that was in the nursing home with me said she was taking me on a trip this week. Do you know when she's picking me up?
Me: I'm not sure mom, we will just have to wait and see.
Mom: okay

Apparently mom is determined to go on a trip!

Mom was in the hospital the past three weeks recovering from a hip replacement (not the nursing home). There was no planned trip or planned flight, it was all in her mind.

I have noticed her thoughts and memories from different times of her life resurface at random times for no particular reason.

May 2, 2017

Making them wrong only confuses them further.

Mom: What's wrong with this remote? *Holding her cell phone*
Me: Try this one. *Handing her the actual TV remote*
Mom: Oh, that's much better! What did you do to fix it?
Me: It's magic!
Mom: Well, I'm glad someone around here has it!

LATER… The Occupational Therapist (OT) arrives

The OT Goes over all the things to do and not to do….don't cross your legs, use the arms of the chair to get up, elevate right leg to reduce swelling…etc.

OT: OKAY, what are you going to do after I leave?
Mom: Well, shit, I didn't know there was going to be a test at the end! I would have paid more attention.
Me: Mom!
Mom: What, "Shit" is my favorite word!
OT: Mine too.

LATER…

Mom: What time is that lady picking me up tomorrow?
Me: What is she picking you up for?

Mom: Some kind of swimming lessons.

Me: I'll have to check on that later. You have a hair appointment tomorrow.

Mom: Well, only if it doesn't interfere with swimming!!

Me: I'll make sure it all works out.

There are no swimming lessons...today, tomorrow or ever!

Every day is an adventure! I believe the trigger for swimming lessons was me cleaning the pool while she sat in a lawn chair, soaking up the sun.

When they confuse words or objects, try to just fix it without really leading them to believe they were "wrong". Instead of saying, "No mom, that is your cell phone, not the remote." I just handed her the remote and took her cell phone and said "Try this one". This way, it doesn't make them feel "wrong" or stupid. They just get mixed up and turned around sometimes.

May 3, 2017

*It's better to not over explain, the more
simple the answer, the better.*

Mom: Where did all these dogs come from?
Me: We adopted them all!
Mom: When?
Me: Over the past 3 years.
Mom: Well, that sure is a lot of dogs. What do you feed them?
Me: Small children...Just kidding!
Mom: Well, wouldn't it be cheaper to feed them dog food?

LATER...

In the car with Chris, mom and myself, on our way home from errands. Chris is driving, mom is in the front seat and I am in the back seat.

Mom: Where is Andrea?
Chris: She's in the back seat.
Mom: Oh, okay. Andrea, where do you need to go now?
Me: I think we will go home now.
Mom: Oh, okay.

LATER...

Mom: Don't we have to pick someone up from church?
Me: I don't think so.
Mom: Well, don't we have to go pick up Chris?
Me: I think Chris is already at home.
Mom: Well you better call him to make sure.
Me: I will after dinner.
Mom: I just know we were supposed to pick someone up for something.
Me: Let me know when you remember who and we will do that.
Mom: Okay

LATER...After dinner

Mom: Where did all these pills come from?
Me: Those are the pills you take after dinner.
Mom: Since when?
Me: For the past 3 years.
Mom: I think you are mistaken, I have never taken this many pills!
Me: How was your dinner?
Mom: Oh it was great, thank you.

We have this same conversation about pills every night, almost verbatim. It's just better to redirect and change the direction of the conversation. They usually don't remember there was ever a disagreement.

May 4, 2017

*An Occupational Therapist (OT) came to the house
today and the conversation was quite humorous!*

OT: Pat, I want you to show me how you are managing your showers.
Mom: What do you mean, how I'm managing showers?
OT: How you are getting in and out of the tub or shower.
Mom: Well I've been managing my whole life just fine without you,
I don't think I need your help now.

I almost fell out of my chair laughing!

Later, we went to see Guardians of the Galaxy.
In the theater well before the previews started...

Mom: Where did Andrea go?
Me: I'm right here mom, I know it's hard to tell because it's so dark,
but I am right next to you.
Mom: OKAY

Coming out of the theater...

Mom: We better wait for Andrea, she was in there too!
Me: I'm here, mom.
Mom: No, the other Andrea, my daughter.

Me: It's okay, she will be along later.
Mom: okay

In the car on the way home.....

Mom: Now, where are we going?
Me: We are going home.
Mom: Where is that? Shiner?
Me: We are going to our house in Georgetown.
Mom: We can't drive that far at night! We better go back to the house in Shiner!
Me: We are in Georgetown, Mom.
Mom: Are you sure? I feel like we drove to Hallettsville to the movie theater.

I called Chris, my son, to help ground her a little, and that seemed to help.

Once we arrived home...

Mom: What movie did you go see?
Me: I went to see Guardians of the Galaxy.
Mom: I think that was what I saw! Where did you sit?
Me: I was right next to you.
Mom: No, Andrea sat next to me!
Me: I need to use the restroom, I'll be right back

Sometimes it helps to leave the room, it almost re-sets their mind/ brain. The days she doesn't recognize me or asks where Andrea is can be heart-breaking. Those are the rough days that make it difficult to sleep and easy to cry. I just do my best to hold it together in front of her so I don't further confuse or upset her. It can be emotionally draining to care for a parent, I feel because of your attachment.

I don't believe I could be a caregiver for a stranger, it's just not a profession I would enjoy. I care for my mom because it's the right thing to do, because I love her and because it's what my dad would have wanted. I often feel guilty for feeling obligated, so I have to remind myself I also do it out of love and respect.

May 5, 2017

Sometimes you have to blame things on the doctor!

This morning....

Mom: Where is everybody?
Me: You and I are here, who are you looking for?
Mom: All the other people that live here...
Me: We have a roommate, Rob, but he isn't here right now.
Mom: What about all the others.
Me: Who else are you thinking about?
Mom: I don't know, I think I was dreaming.
Me: It's okay, sometimes dreams can seem really real!

This afternoon...

We ran a few errands

Me: Hold on a second, let me get your walker out of the back seat.
Mom: Oh, I don't need it today.
Me: The Dr. said you need to use it for a few months.
Mom: Oh, that Dr. doesn't know what he's talking about, I don't need a silly walker. I've been walking without one all my life, why would I need one now?
Me: You had a hip replacement a month ago, you need it to keep your balance, just for a while, not forever.

Mom: Fine!

This evening..... Dinner time

Mom: Where is that other lady?
Me: What other lady?
Mom: That lady that cooks for us.
Me: That's me! I cook for us.
Mom: OKAY, I'm Pat, right?
Me: Yes Ma'am.
Mom: You are Andrea?
Me: Yes Ma'am
Mom: Are you Andrea, my daughter?
Me: Yes Ma'am, I am your daughter.
Mom: OKAY, I was just checking, seems like the rules and people keep changing around here.

The Alzheimer's brain is not always rational and THAT sucks! At least that's the case with my mom. My Roommate said his patient can be very rational at times, so I imagine every case is different in that aspect. I believe it also has to do with the stage they are in. I said it before, and I'll say it again... Their reality is not the same reality as yours, you have to fit into their world or their reality in order to make them feel safe, secure and less confused.

May 6, 2017

*Remember, you need to take breaks from being
a caregiver, even if only for a few hours.*

I had been gone all morning (Southwestern University Graduation!)
Chris, my son, stayed with mom so I could attend. Thank you.

After Chris left, mom and I were alone at the house.

Mom: Where were you all day?
Me: I went to Southwestern to watch some of my friends graduate!
Mom: Well are you going to stay here awhile.
Me: Yes Ma'am.
Mom: You shouldn't have been gone so long, I had no idea where
you were.
Me: Okay.

Later this afternoon...

Me: Mom, will you come with me to run a few errands?
Mom: Okay. It sure beats sitting here watching the walls dry!
Me; Are you ready?
Mom: I will be in a few.

Mom walks to her room, I am assuming to brush her hair and get
her purse.

15+ minutes later.....

Me: Are you ready?
Mom: Ready for what?
Me: To go run errands.
Mom: Well, I didn't know that was what you were going to do, why didn't you say something.

Surprise...Not really.

This evening......

My back has been hurting the past few days so I told mom I was going to lay down for a while. About 5 minutes later she comes into my room.

Mom: Are you staying here tonight?
Me: Yes Ma'am
Mom: OKAY, good, I don't want to you drive back this late.
Me: Yes ma'am

I guess she forgot we were at my house....

It's almost always better to go with the flow, and not correct a person with Alzheimer's, it just confuses them more and makes them feel like they are crazy. It can be more frustrating for the caregiver than the person with Alzheimer's!

May 7, 2017

I realize I repeat myself sometimes, but I feel some things are so important they need to be mentioned more than once!

This afternoon, mom and I watched a movie in my room.

Mom: Andrea, who's room are we in?
Me: This is my room.
Mom: Why don't you have carpet in your room?
Me: I took out the carpet and stained the concrete so it's easier to clean. Having 5 dogs with carpet in my room wouldn't be good.
Mom: I guess you are right.

Today was a good day. She was a little less confused than usual.

This evening... 20 minutes after we ate dinner

Mom: What are we having for dinner tonight?
Me: We already had dinner. You wanted cereal, so we ate cereal.
Mom: I don't anymore remember that than a man in the moon!
Me: Are you still hungry? I can make you something else.
Mom: Well, no, if we already ate, I don't want to eat again!
Me: Okay

Sundowning....is brutal! Sundowning is a symptom of Alzheimer's disease and some dementia patients. When it's dusk, it is a bit harder to see, which can cause confusion. I have noticed it happens less to mom when I turn the lights on in the house just before dusk, that way it doesn't really get dark in the house until it's time to go to bed. If her hall light is off after dark, she asks me to turn it on for her before she gets to the dark area. I have also noticed a new fear of the dark with mom. I usually turn on her bedroom light before she even asks because it just eliminates that anxiety before it has a chance to set in.

May 8, 2017

*Some days are more confusing than others…
the day of the week especially!*

Mom: Is today Sunday?

Me: Today is Monday.

Mom: Well, this newspaper says Sunday.

Me: I was about to go outside to get today's paper.

Mom: Okay. Then that will make it Monday, right?

Me: Yes ma'am.

I brought the paper in from the driveway…

Mom: Well, where did you get that?

Me: It was in the driveway, we have it delivered every morning so you have a paper to read.

Mom: Since when?

Me: For the past 3 years since you moved in.

Mom: I don't live here, I'm just a guest!

Me: I'll be back, I need to go feed the dogs and cats.

This evening before dinner…..

Me: I need to feed the dogs and cats before our dinner is ready.

Mom: Did you make enough for all the kids?

Me: What kids?

Mom: All the kids we have here.

Me: You mean the fur babies/kids?

Mom: Don't be ridiculous! I mean the human kids!

Me: Where are they?

Mom: I don't know, wherever you are keeping them.

Me: I think they all went home.

Mom: Oh, so we don't have to feed them?

Me: Nope, they are all taken care of.

Mom: okay

There were no kids at the house!

After dinner...

Mom: Now, where am I sleeping tonight?

Me: In your room, just around that corner.

Mom: Well, I don't have anything to sleep in!

Me: I'm sure we can find something in your room.

Mom: I doubt that! I wish you would have told me we were staying. *Getting agitated* I didn't pack a suitcase or anything!

Me: Mom, it's okay, you live here.

Mom: Why don't I remember that?

Me: Because you have Alzheimer's.

Mom: Oh.

We don't have any kids in the house, so I'm not sure where she got that idea. I have noticed that when she watches something on TV, she sometimes confuses that with reality. I try to stick to gameshows and limit her TV time to cut down on confusion.

Keeping mom in the present moment also helps. If I bring up future events, she will obsess about them or worry about missing something. Bringing up past events can also trigger confusion and anxiety with mom, so I try to avoid that as well. Talking about the here and now almost always has a positive outcome.

I can usually gauge if telling her the truth will be well received by the mood she is in. Sometimes it works, sometimes it doesn't. She doesn't remember it by the next day anyway, so it's a clean slate.

It's always tough when she asks where she's sleeping or when she's going home. Even though she has been living with me for the past three years, she still gets very confused about where she is and why she is here.

May 9, 2017

Reassurance is key to keeping them calm!

Mom: I have just about everything packed, so I'm ready to go when you are.
Me: Where are we going?
Mom: Home.
Me: We are home.
Mom: No we aren't, we are just here visiting.
Me: All of your things are here, we have both lived here for the past 2 years.
Mom: Well someone told me to pack all of my things. Who told me to pack?
Me: I think you fell asleep and had a dream about that.
Mom: I don't think so. I know someone told me to pack!
Me: It's okay, sometimes dreams seem really real.

I checked her room for packed bags to be sure she didn't really pack her things up. Nothing was packed, no suitcases were out, so I do believe she had a dream she was packing up.

Later in the afternoon...... Mom went to lay down, so I went to rest my back in my room...

About 15 minutes later mom came into my room looking very confused.

Mom: Andrea, are you alright?

Me: Yes, I'm okay other than my back hurting.

Mom: Someone just came into my room and just started putting all my clothes in plastic bags and told me I needed to get out. I don't know where they went, but they are coming back, so they said.

Me: Let's go take a look in your room.

We walk back to mom's room and nothing is in plastic bags. Everything is in its place.

Me: I think you were dreaming, mom. All of your clothes are in your closet along with your shoes. And all of your P.J.'s are in the drawer along with everything else.

Mom: Well, I just must be losing my mind!

Me: It was just a very realistic dream. It's okay, that happens to me too sometimes.

Mom: Well, I feel better now, thank you!

After dinner ......

Mom: Where is that lady we came here with today?

Me: I'm not sure who you are talking about.

Mom: The lady that drove us here from Houston.

Me: Oh, she went home.

Mom: Well is she coming back to get us to take us back.

Me: I think we will stay here for now.

Mom: We need to get back tonight.

Me: I need to do the dishes.

I have noticed more and more confusion as the days pass and her Alzheimer's progresses. It's very difficult to watch and even harder to deal with emotionally. When she wakes up scared or upset, I try calming her by showing her or taking her to the source of confusion.

It comforts her when I show physical evidence that confirms what I am telling her.

I believe mom relives past events in her life. I remember stories she told me about taking trips to Houston when she was a young woman. She had a friend, Dorothy, which she would ride with to and from Houston when she still lived in Shiner. So when she asks where Dorothy is or the lady she rode here with, I believe her mind is going back to that time in her life. Even though it's sad at times, she seems at peace when she talks about her travels, even if she is confused with the timeline.

May 10, 2017

As difficult as it can be sometimes, be patient.

Me: Are you ready to go, mom?

Mom: Where are we going?

Me: To get your hair done at the beauty shop.

Mom: Well, you didn't tell me we were going today.

We go EVERY Wednesday! AND I told her 30 minutes prior to this conversation

Mom's Occupational Therapist (OT) came today to make sure she was getting in and out of the tub safely.

OT: Pat, let's take a shower, okay?

Mom: No, I don't need to take a shower, I took one last night. *No, she didn't.*

OT: I need to make sure you are getting in and out of the tub safely.

Mom: I am, my daughter helps me. When she gets back, you can ask her. *I was sitting right there.*

Me: Mom, you showered on Sunday, you need to shower tonight.

Mom: Well, I'll do it later, I'm too cold right now.

OT: We will put the heater on for you.

Me: I've turned the heater on in the bathroom for you.

Mom: How, we were out of matches yesterday.

Me: I bought some this afternoon.

Mom: *Looking at the OT.* – I'll take a shower if you take your clothes off too.

OT: I don't think my boss would think that was very professional. *She had a great sense of humor about it, thank goodness!*

Me: OKAY, mom, let's get this done.

Mom: Well, shit, whatever will make you two happy and shut the hell up about showering!

Ahhhhhh…the joys of having your parent living with you…

Later in the evening…

Mom: What time is mother picking us up?

Me: I didn't know she was coming, are you sure that's today?

Mom: Well I thought it was today.

Me: I don't think she is coming today.

Mom: Oh, okay.

Talk about a blast from the past! Her mom died before I was even born. Both of her parents died before Alzheimer's disease had a chance to take them over. Her sister did die from complications of Alzheimer's so it's probable that it runs in the family. Makes me a bit thankful that I am adopted!

May 11, 2017

"Going home" seems to be a bit of an obsession.

Mom: When are we going home?
Me: We are home.
Mom: I thought we were at the beach!
Me: I wish we were at the beach! That sounds like fun
Mom: Well, why did I think we were at the beach?
Me: You have Alzheimer's, so you get mixed up sometimes, but that's why I'm here.
Mom: Well, I sure am glad you are here to keep things straight!

Mom: Where are all my clothes?
Me: In your closet.
Mom: Where is that?
Me: In your bedroom.
Mom: Where is my bedroom?
Pointing to the hallway toward her bedroom
Me: It's around the corner, down the hall.
Mom: How long has that been my room?
Me: For the past 2 years.
Mom: Huh, okay.

Mom: How long are we staying here?
Me: For a while, we do live here.
Mom: Since when?

Me: For the past 2 years.
Mom: I think you are pulling my leg!
Me: How about an Oreo?
Mom: Oh, I never turn down an Oreo! Thank you.

Mom travels so very often, I sometimes wish I had that ability! I have noticed she will drift off, not completely asleep, but in a relaxed state. I believe this is when she dreams or reminisces about times past. When she becomes more aware of her surroundings and realizes they don't match what she was thinking about, she gets very confused. That must be so frightening for her! Once I ground her and give her the information about the here and now, she usually comes out of it.

May 12, 2017

*Bonding time is important. You change your
role when you become a caregiver!*

This morning...

Mom: Did you let the others know we were leaving this morning?
Mom and I are the only ones here...
Me: We won't go anywhere until this afternoon.
Mom: Oh, I thought we were leaving this morning.
Me: I need to clean the house, then go to the bank, will you go with me?
Mom: Sure, I can go to the bank with you.
This afternoon we went to a nail place. I wanted to get our nails done for Mother's day.
Mr. Woo: Ms. Pat, can I polish your nails today?
Mom: Well, I guess so, if you want to. I just came in with that lady over there.
Mr. Woo: Is that your daughter?
Mom: Well, that's what she keeps telling everyone, so I guess so.

This evening I made grilled cheese sandwiches for dinner...

Mom: What's this?
Me: Dinner. I made grilled cheese sandwiches.
Mom: Oh, goodness! I haven't had a grilled cheese sandwich in years

34

She had one last week...

Mom slept some today while I cleaned house, hopefully she sleeps tonight. Mom did seem to enjoy getting her nails done. She especially loved that they were RED!!!.

Thanks, Katie, for suggesting to add pictures to the posts!

May 13, 2017

Delusions are sometimes part of daily life!

Mom: Who are we missing?

Me: I don't think we are missing anyone.

Mom: What about that lady that rode with us earlier?

Me: She went home in her car.

There was no one else with us. I believe she drifted off into her own little world and had a dream we were with others.

Chris got us some of the best chocolate in the world (Frans)!!! We had both had a couple of pieces a few minutes earlier....

Mom: Do we have any candy, or chocolate?

Me: Yes ma'am, Chris bought us that wonderful chocolate candy! Would you like another piece?

Mom: When did he give us chocolate? I haven't had any!

Me: Here ya go... *Letting her pick out another piece of candy, not saying any more about when we got it and that it was her third piece in the last 15 minutes. Stating a fact outside her reality just confuses her more, so I try to avoid that.*

Me: Let's take a picture together!

Mom: Where is the camera?

Me: My phone is the camera.

Mom: Don't be silly. You can't take a picture with a phone!

Me: Watch.......Smile.....

I show her the picture.....

Mom: Well, I'll be!!! Where do you get them developed?
Me: I can send them to the printer and print one right now!
Mom: Okay, NOW you are pulling my leg for sure!

Her innocence and absence of knowledge for technology cracks me up! I can only imagine it must be like living in the Jetsons world for her sometimes!

May 14, 2017

Every day is a new challenge.

Mom: I'm going to go get the paper.
Me: I'll come with you.
Mom: Well then you go get it.
Me: It's a beautiful day, we should both go.
Mom: Well if you insist, fine! I don't need this walker, do I?
Me: Yes ma'am, the Dr. wants you to take it everywhere for a few months.
Mom: Well that Dr. doesn't know what he's talking about.

Me: Happy Mother's day, Mom.
Mom: Why would you say that, I'm not your mom.
Me: Yes, you are my mom. I am your daughter.
Mom: Well, yes, you are my daughter.
Me: I love you mom.
Mom: That's nice.

Mom: when are we going back to Houston?
Me: I think we will stay here, since we live here.
Mom: Since when?
Me: For the past 2 years.
Mom: Well, I don't remember that.
Me: Here are your pills, mom.
Mom: My heavens! What are all these for?

Me: These are what the Dr. prescribed for you.
Mom: Well, that's just too many!

Happy Mother's day to all my friends who are Moms to human children and furry children!

May 15, 2017

Find the humor every chance you can!

Me: Here's you breakfast, mom.
Mom: Well I didn't know you were making breakfast!
I make her breakfast every morning!
Mom: Where are my marbles?
Me: *Almost falling out of my chair laughing!* Well, I am not sure, where did you last see them?
Mom: Well, I was playing with them earlier, but can't find them now.

I have marbles I use for crafting, so I found a little velvet bag and put a few in the bag and took them to her. Took maybe 5 minutes….

Me: Here ya go, mom.
Mom: What's this?
Me: The marbles you were looking for.
Mom: I wasn't looking for any marbles!

Some days I feel like it's ME losing my mind…. This was one of the funniest interactions we have had in a while. I couldn't stop laughing at one point, and mom was looking at me like I was nuts, which made me laugh even harder.…I had to leave the room!

Me: Here's some cake!
Mom: Where did that come from?

Me: I made it.

Mom: When did you learn how to bake?

Me: You taught me!

Mom: You didn't learn that from me! I've never baked a cake in my life!

Mom always baked my birthday cakes

May 16, 2017

Sone days are more challenging than others.

We went to see Chris today to help him paint a wall. It was so fun to visit!

Mom: Did you bring in those stones from the car?
Me: What stones?
Chris: What did you forget to bring in?
Mom: Those stones, but she (pointing to me) will lie about it, she always lies.

Mom: Are we kin?
Me: Yes, I am your daughter, you are my mother.
Mom: I must be losing my mind, I don't remember that!
Me: It's okay mom, I'm here to remind you of that.
Mom: I sure am sorry.

Mom: Where are we going now?
Me: We are headed home.
Mom: Who's home?
Me: Our home, in Georgetown.
Mom: I don't live in Georgetown, I live in Houston.
Me: We have lived together in Georgetown for the past 3 years.
Mom: Are you sure?
Me: Yes ma'am.

Mom: Why don't I remember that?

Me: You have Alzheimer's, but it's Okay because I am here to keep everything straight for you.

I am exhausted today....Some days are more draining than others. Today is one of those days. But it was so great to see my kiddo!!!

May 17, 2017

Peat and repeat.

Mom: Is today Friday?
Me: Today is Wednesday.
Mom: Are you sure?
Me: What day do you go to the beauty shop?
Mom: I think Wednesday.
Me: That's right. Did you get your hair done today?
Mom: I don't know, did I?
Me: Yes, an hour ago.

Five minutes later......

Mom: Is today Saturday?
Me: Today is Wednesday.
Mom: That's what I thought.

About an hour later.....

Mom: Is today Saturday or Sunday?
Me: Did you enjoy your dinner? Was the turkey moist enough?
Mom: Oh yes, dinner was great!

Sometimes she gets stuck in a loop and changing the subject often breaks the loop, or cycle. Sometimes asking the question back works too. The odd thing about Alzheimer's is…What works today, may not work later, or tomorrow. It's a day by day disease.

Mom: Where are the girls I came here with?
Me: The girls?
Mom: Did they go back?
Me: I guess so, they aren't here.
Mom: OKAY.
Mom: Why does my hip hurt?
Me: You had a hip replacement about a month ago, so it's going to be a little sore. I gave you a pain pill with dinner, so it should feel better soon.
Mom: I don't remember having surgery. Was I in the hospital?
Me: No Mom, they did it here on the dining room table. Yes, you were in the hospital.
Mom: Well, I sure don't remember that.
Me: Would you like some ice cream?
Mom: Yes, that sounds good.

May 18, 2017

Short-term memory goes first!

Mom: Why do people keep coming here to ask me how I am?
Me: That was the nurse for Physical Therapy making sure you are doing better and to see if you are ready for discharge. You had a hip replacement and they want to make sure you are healing properly. Yesterday, the Physical Therapist was here to do your exercises with you.
Mom: Well, I hope they don't come back, it's not necessary for them to come here.
Me: They just want to make sure you are safe. They care about you.
Mom: Well, that's enough now.

Mom: I've been thinking about getting a car, but have decided I'm just going to keep walking.
Me: I can drive you.

We all had a good chuckle at that!

Later, after we arrived home...

Mom: Whose house is this and why are we here?
Me: This is our house, we have been living here for two years now.
Mom: How did that happen?
Me: I bought a house and we moved in.

Mom: Oh, well, I was just wondering.

Mom: What are our big plans for the evening?

Me: I thought we would stay in and relax.

Mom: well that doesn't sound like fun, let's go do something.

Me: What would you like to do?

Mom: I don't know.

Me: Well let me know when you think of something.

Mom: That's your job. To figure out what to do.

She can be really funny sometimes! Sometimes the smallest of suggestions can be very helpful and I hope you all have a great evening!

Mom doesn't look too happy in these pictures, but she had a really great time!

May 19, 2017

Sometimes the journey in their mind is so vivid to them!

Mom: What did I learn this morning?
Me: I'm not sure, where did you go this morning?
Mom: I went to the town meeting but I don't remember what they talked about.
Me: I think you had a dream, we have been home all morning.
Mom: Are you sure?
Me: Yes ma'am.
Mom: Well, it sure seemed real!

Mom: Where did we go earlier?
Me: We went outside to get the paper.
Mom: No, after that.
Me: We went back inside after we watched the deer for a while.
Mom: Well, you don't have to make up stories, don't be stupid!

Me: Mom, you need your walker.
Mom: No I don't, I'll just hold on to you.
Me: I don't want you to fall again, let me get your walker, just a second.
Mom: I said I don't need it you stupid girl!

Me: Mom, please don't talk to me like that.
Mom: I'm older than you, I'll talk to you however I want!

Rough day today.

The picture was taken before all the meanness from her today.

May 20, 2017

Redirect, redirect, redirect

Me: Did you hear that storm last night?

Mom: No, I didn't hear a thing!

Me: It was thundering so loud it shook the whole house!

Mom: Well next time there is a storm like that, wake me up.

It was around midnight. I don't think I'll wake her at that time of the night! I figure if she sleeps that soundly, let her sleep. That might change as the disease progresses. There are some reports of Alzheimer's patients wandering later in the progression of the disease and they had never wandered or awakened in the night before.

Mom: I think I'm going home tomorrow.

Me: You are home, mom.

Mom: Since when?

Me: You have lived with me for three years.

Mom: Why?

Me: Did you like that blueberry cake?

Mom: Yes, that was good. Where did you get it?

Me: I made it!

Mom: You don't know how to cook.

I cook at least twice a day...... Oh, and I made that blueberry lemon cake that someone posted on facebook today and it was AMAZING!

Mom: What do we do all day?

Me: Well, it depends on the day.
Mom: Do I have a job?
Me: No, ma'am, you are retired.
Mom: Retired from what?
Me: Being a full time mom and housewife.
Mom: Well, do I travel?
Me: Sometimes.
Mom: How do I get there?
Me: I take you.
Mom: Why don't I have a car?
Me: You don't need one, I take you places you need to go. You don't drive any more.
Mom: Well I could, I know how!

While I was cooking dinner, mom disappeared into her room. I went to get her when dinner was ready....I found her packing her suitcase. This was too funny not to share...

Me: Hey mom, dinner is ready. Are you going somewhere?
Mom: Yes, I'm going home. I just don't trust all these people that are coming in and out of the house.
Me: What people?
Mom: You don't pay attention to anything, do you?
Me: Come on, let's go eat before our dinner gets cold.
Mom: Okay.

While mom was cleaning up her dishes, I unpacked her suitcase and put everything away.......She forgot all about packing.

The baby deer was in the front yard this morning....so precious!

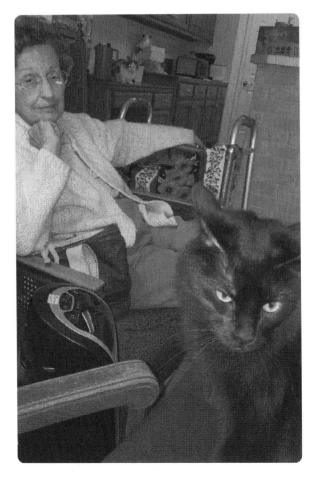

Me: Did you hear that!
Mom: What was that?
Me: That was thunder!
Mom: No, I think that's someone down the hall playing their music too loud.
Me: Mom, look outside, it's raining.
Mom: I guess so.
Mom: What are you doing in here?

*I was sewing in the dining room....the table is big, so it gives me a lot of space.

Me: I am sewing a quilt.
Mom: Why?
Me: Because I promised someone I would make them one.
Mom: That sure seems like a lot of trouble when you can just go buy one.
Me: I love to sew.
Mom: Well you sure didn't get that from me! I don't think I can even thread a needle!

8:30 this evening......

Mom: I think I'll have a cup of coffee.
Me: Mom, it's 8:30...PM...
Mom: No, that's AM, not PM.....You are crazy!!!
Me: It will keep you up all night.
Mom: OKAY....Miss know it all.... Whatever you say....

May 22, 2017

Sometimes you have to decide for them.

Me: What would you like for lunch?
Mom: Oh, I don't know, what are the others having?
Me: Sandwiches.
Mom: Well, that's what I'll have.

*There were no others ....

*8PM.....I was sewing in the dining room and mom walks in

Mom: I'm going to bed.
Me: Are you okay?
Mom: I think so, why?
Me: well, it's only eight O'clock....
Mom: No, it's much later than that!
Me: Oh, okay. Good night.

It's best not to press issues with mom. Sometimes she goes into her room and forgets she was going to bed and comes out again to watch TV or talk with me.

May 23, 2017

Their dreams often become their reality.

Mom: What are you doing in there?
Me: I'm making lunch.
Mom: I thought we were going to a picture show.

*We never talked about going to a movie.

Me: I'm making you a grilled ham and cheese sandwich.
Mom: Well, don't make too much, I'm not that hungry.

Later in the afternoon.....We were sitting in the breakfast area watching some TV....I'm pretty sure mom fell asleep...

Mom: Where have you been? I have been looking everywhere for you!
Me: Well, you found me.
Mom: Don't run off like that again!
Me: Would you like a piece of cake?
Mom: Are you having a piece?
Me: I sure am.
Mom: Well, I can't let you eat desert alone!
Mom cracks me up sometimes!

May 24, 2017

Reassurance is key!

Mom: When should we start packing?
Me: Where are we going?
Mom: Back to Houston.
Me: Not today.
Mom: That's right, we live here now, don't we?
Me: That's right
Mom: I feel like I am losing my mind!
Me: It's okay, mom, that's why I'm here.

Me: Dinner is ready.
Mom: Oh, I didn't know you were cooking.
Me: Well, we have to eat ;-)
Mom: I didn't know you knew how to cook!

*I cook every night and every night, she is surprised....

Mom: I think I fell asleep in the chair.
Me: That's okay. Do you want to go lay down on your bed?
Mom: My bed isn't here and I don't want to sleep in some other person's bed!

Me: OKAY mom.

I was so tired all day today, I forgot to take a picture, so here is Sasha, sleeping in bed....

May 25, 2017

Mom and I had an early start on errands today, one of which was at Hobby Lobby. This was our conversation while getting out of the car.

Mom: Wait a minute now, it's so windy, I can't see a thing!
Me: I didn't know wind affected your sight! Ha!
Mom: Well, it's so bright I can't see.

*Once we were inside….

Mom: Now I really can't see!
Me: Take off your sunglasses.
Mom: *Taking off her sunglasses…Oh, that's much better! I thought that wind was going to blow us away.
Me: It was pretty windy!

On our way to dinner with Sheri today…….

Mom: What are we going to do about the dog we picked up?
Me: What dog?
Mom: The one in the back seat.
Me: *Looking back there…I don't think he's there anymore.
Mom: Well, you're right, he's gone. Where did he go?
Me: He went home.
Mom: Oh, okay.

*There was never a dog in the back seat (At least not today.)

I decided to try Blue Bell's Brides Cake Ice cream (AMAZING!!!)

Me: Here, mom, try this.
Mom: What is this?
Me: Try it, it's a surprise!
Mom: Oh, my goodness! That's so good! You should be ashamed of yourself for giving me this much!
Me: I'll eat what you can't.
Mom: Like hell you will!

Ha ha ha ha ha ha….yup….still spunky! 88 and still going….

May 26, 2017

Mom, my roomie, Rob and I all went to run errands this morning and there were many funny, and confusing conversations! Enjoy the beautiful madness!

We have been in the car for about half an hour......

Mom: Do you mind if I ask a question?
Me: Of course not, what's up?
Mom: Where in the hell are you taking me?
Me: (Chuckling) We are going to San Marcos.
Mom: Why?
Me: To pick up a truck and have lunch.
Mom: Well that's a long drive to get lunch!

Later....

Mom: What time does that parade start?
Me: What parade?
Mom: The one you have been talking about since we got here.

*Clearly there was no parade...we were sitting at a Starbucks enjoying a relaxing afternoon.

Rob: Maybe we will check it out later
Mom: OKAY, that's all I asked.

As we were leaving, I placed mom's walker in front of her...she walked around it. I put it in front of her again and said...

Me: Mom, you need to use your walker.

Mom: That's not mine.

Me: Yes it is.

Mom: I've never seen that in my life.

Me: Mom, please use it, the Dr. wants you to use it wherever you go.

Mom: Well, I certainly don't remember that, are you sure you're not making that up. You have always liked making up stories...

Me: No, mom, I am not making anything up.

May 27, 2017

Today was a bit of a challenge.….some days are.

Mom: When are we leaving for that meeting?
Me: What meeting?
Mom: The meeting I told you about.
Me: We aren't going to that today, that's sometime next week. How about we go see a movie.

*There was never any meeting.….

Mom: I guess so.

After waking up from a nap…

Mom: Where is my purse?
Me: It's probably in your room.
Mom: No, I already looked there. I hope that maid didn't take it.

*We don't have a maid……

Me: I'll go check your room.
Mom: You can check all you want, but it's not there!
Me: Here it is.
Mom: Where was it?
Me: In your room.
Mom: I figured that's where it was.

Mom: Where is my phone?
Me: Probably in your purse, or your pocket.
Mom: No, I already looked.
Me: Look again, I thought I saw you put it in your purse.

*Mom digs around in her purse for 5 – 10 minutes.

Mom: What am I looking for?
Me: Your phone.
Mom: No, that's not it. I think it was something else.
Me: I have no idea.

The last two conversations usually occur 5 – 10+ times a day....
seriously. Some days feel like Groundhog Day....(The movie)

May 28, 2017

Fewer moments of clarity.

Mom: I can't finish this other half of the sandwich, what should I do with it?
Me: I'll take care of it.
Mom: What are you going to do with it?
Me: Probably throw it away.
Mom: Don't do that, someone in the wilderness could eat it.
Me: I don't think we have a wilderness…ha ha ha
Mom: Doesn't someone live in the woods in the back yard?
Me: I sure hope not!
Mom: Well I sure thought they did.

*Sometimes I feel like I've walked into the middle of very strange conversation….

Mom: Did my sister get her school stuff taken care of?

*I paused and looked at her for a minute to see if she would snap back. Nope.

Mom: Why are you looking at me like that?
Me: Mom, your sister passed away over a year ago.
Mom: Oh, that's right. I guess I just don't want to remember that.

Me: Would you rather I tell you the truth, or would you rather I just agree with you?
Mom: I guess whatever you think I should hear at that given time.

I was really surprised at her answer. A very thoughtful statement.

I have noticed mom sometimes has these moments of clarity and speaks to me as there is no illness, no Alzheimer's. These moments are becoming less and less frequent as her disease progresses, but truly treasured when they do!

May 29, 2017

Try not to ask confusing or complex questions.

Mom: Who's house are we in right now?
Me: Our house.
Mom: No, I think it's Andrea's
Me: Who am I?
Mom: *Taking a long pause…. Well, I think you are Andrea.
Me: Yes, that's right. Do you know how we are related?
Mom: That's too much to think about.
Me: I think I will make rice and shrimp tonight, how does that sound? Or would you rather have potatoes?
Mom: Rice sounds much better, you don't have to peel rice.

She cracks me up!!!!!

The picture is of the back side of the quilt I am making. Just finished that today….tomorrow, I will put it all together!

May 30, 2017

Sometimes you have to ignore a question altogether.

Mom: What are we doing today?
Me: What would you like to do today?
Mom: I don't know, but I do know we have to go to work soon. Is that what you are wearing to work?

*I was still in my P.J.'s

Me: I'll make us breakfast before we decide what to do. Eggs and toast okay?
Mom: That sounds fine.

*I made breakfast and she forgot all about "going to work"

This afternoon my son Chris called and we talked for a while, then he talked to mom. I left the room so I had no idea what was said.

Me: I'm going to start dinner. How does chicken strips, mashed potatoes and broccoli sound?
Mom: Well, I thought we were leaving.
Me: Where are we going?
Mom: To the movies!
Me: We aren't going to the movies tonight.
Mom: Yes we are!

Me: Okay. After we eat dinner.
Mom: Well you better let the others know we aren't going.

*I called Chris to see if he mentioned us all going to the movies on Sunday, and he had. Sometimes telling mom about future plans can get very mixed up in her mind. I spent the next hour trying to convince her we weren't going until Sunday...ha ha ha! This has happened before.....telling her of future plans, then she keeps asking when we are going and almost obsessing over it.

Today was a bit rough. I thought about my dad a lot and that helped me through the day. The call from my kiddo helped even more.

Mia had to get in the picture with us....she's a silly girl

May 31, 2017

Mom: Where is everybody this morning?
Me: We are both here. Who else are you looking for?
Mom: Everyone else that lives here!
Me: Rob is at work, he's the only other person that lives here.
Mom: No, there are others that live here, like that woman that cooks for us and that other lady that cleans house.
Me: Mom, that's me. I cook and clean.
Mom: Well I don't know how you keep up. I guess it just seems like more people live here.

I took mom to her weekly beauty shop trip, which she always enjoys. The picture is of us and our hair lady, Sarah

We also went to lunch with a dear friend of mine.

Mom: I have no idea what I want for lunch. What are you having?
Me: I am going to have migas. Let's look at the menu to see what looks good......How about the breakfast platter?
Mom: Yes, that looks good.

A couple of minutes later.......

Mom: I have no idea what I want for lunch. What are you having?
Me: I think you decided on the breakfast platter.

Mom: I think that sounds good.

*This went on until the waiter came for our order.

June 1, 2017

Sometimes you need time to yourself.

Mom: I have some laundry to do. Should I give it to you or take it home with me and do it there?

Me: Mom, you are home.

Mom: I know. I was just pretending I was going home.

*Mom brings me her clothes that she needs me to wash....

Mom: NOW can I go home!

*I just hugged her and said, "I'm glad you live here too."

Today was a good day! Mom was in a good mood and I was able to clean house and sew with few interruptions! I even started on a new quilt!

June 2, 2017

Alzheimer's is so unfair.

Mom: Who's that in the back yard?
Me: That's Rob and his son.
Mom: Who's Rob?
Me: Our roommate and his son.
Mom: When did he move in?
Me: A year ago.
Mom: Oh. Well why didn't you tell me? I didn't know that.
Mom: What time is that meeting today?
Me: There isn't a meeting today.
Mom: I think you're mistaken.
Me: I think you have your days mixed up.
Mom: Maybe.

*There is no meeting....

A lot of repetition today...more so than usual. I did manage to finish the top half of a new quilt I'm making.

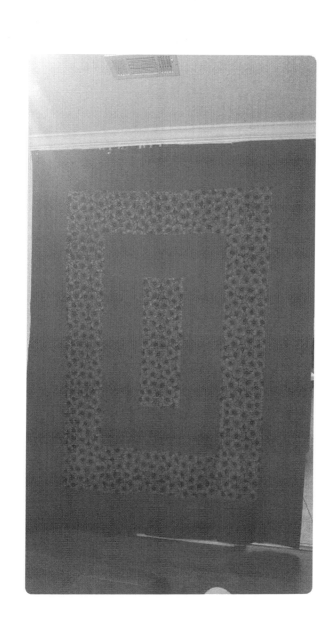

June 3, 2017

There is a definite fear of water with Alzheimer's.

Mom: Where are we going?
Me: To hobby lobby.
Mom: What for?
Me: I need a few things to finish the two quilts I'm working on.

*We had this very same conversation at the house before we left and 3 times in the car on the way to hobby lobby.

Me: Mom, you need to shower tonight.
Mom: No I don't, I showered last night.
Me: no you didn't.
Mom: How do you know, you weren't here.
Me: Yes I was, and I promise, you didn't.
Mom: Fine. You think you know everything.

*She stomped off to the bathroom and took a 5 minute shower....

Mom hasn't wanted her picture taken the past few days. Hopefully she will tomorrow! We are going to go see Chris and the Wonder Woman movie!

Showering has become more and more difficult. I have read that it's common for Alzheimer patients to develop a fear or aversion to water or showering. I know my mom won't shower unless I tell her she needs to. Even then, sometimes she refuses.

Daily challenges can be exhausting and leave you feeling defeated. Be sure to make time for yourself, it's imperative! Someone reminded me, you have to take care of yourself before you can take care of someone else. That is so true! It reminds me of flight attendants telling you to put your own oxygen mask on first, in case of an emergency. There is so much truth in that, mentally as well as physically!

June 4, 2017

I got up at 7AM this morning and got mom up at 8. This is the only way I can get things done before I wake her up. …. Feed the cats and dogs, sweep my room and kitchen, etc.

Me: Mom, it's time to wake up.
Mom: What on earth for, it's only 8AM!!!
Me: We are going to see a movie.
Mom: You'll have to go without me, it's too early!
Me: We are going to go see Chris.
Mom: Well, why didn't you say so? I'll be ready in less than an hour.

On the way home mom asked me the same question ….over and over and over….

Mom: Where's my suitcase?
Me: We were only at Chris's house for a few hours, so you didn't take a suitcase.
Mom: Then why do I remember packing a bag?
Me: I have no idea, mom.
Mom: I need a washcloth and some pajamas for tonight, if we are staying here.
Me: The washcloths are in your bathroom and your PJs are in your bedroom.
Mom: don't have a bedroom here.
Me: Let me show you.

*We walk into her room.....

Mom: Well these are my things, but this isn't my house.

*I had to walk away.......I am exhausted after the past few days....
Just exhausted......

June 5, 2017

Some days are like a hamster wheel!

Mom: What is today?
Me: Monday. Look at your paper.
Mom: When is hair day?
Me: Wednesday at noon. Look at the calendar next to you.

*This conversation happened at least 20 times within a 2 hour span. I am not sure what set this cycle in motion, but redirecting did not help this morning!! I tried all my tricks, even going outside to change the scenery! Just a rough morning.

Mom: What is today?
Me: Mom, I can't answer that again. Look at your paper, it has the date.

*There was a 30 second pause.....

Mom: Is today Monday?
Me: Yes, mom.
Mom: Is hair day Wednesday?
Me: Yes, mom.
Mom: Should I take a shower tomorrow night.
Me: Yes ma'am.
Mom: OKAY

The repetition of the same questions is a daily occurrence, and sometimes unbearable, but you just answer the same questions over and over and over. It's exhausting!

On a positive note, I am almost finished with one of the quilts!

June 6, 2017

*I brought the newspaper in and she had been reading it for about half an hour.

Me: What are you up to?
Mom: Oh, just studying for exams.
Me: What exams?
Mom: English, History and all the other usual exams you have to take at the end of the year.
Me: Oh, OKAY.

*I had to leave the room to prevent her from seeing me chuckle.

Mom: Why the hell can't I remember anything?
Me: Because you have Alzheimer's.
Mom: Well, that isn't good. When did that happen?
Me: Three years ago.
Mom: Is that how long I've been living with you?
Me: Yes Ma'am. I wish I could fix it.
Mom: Well, that's just one of those things, I guess.
Me: I'm so sorry mom.
Mom: It's okay. I'm just glad you are able to let me stay here with you.

Some days are pretty great....sad, but great.

I am pet sitting for a really sweet lady with two cats and one really took a liking to mom.

June 7, 2017

Mom was out of sorts today making today difficult.

I took mom to get her hair done today and she refused to use her walker.

Me: Hang on, mom, let me get your walker from the back.
Mom: I don't need that thing.
Me: The Dr. says you need to use it so you don't lose your balance.
Mom: No. I don't want to use it.

*I placed the walker in front of her so she would use it. She gives me a very dirty look....

Mom: I said I don't need it.
Me: Please use the walker, I may not be able to catch you if you lost your balance.
Mom: Anything to shut you up!
Me: Are you hungry for anything in particular for lunch?
Mom: I'll just eat at school today.

*I made her a turkey sandwich and she never mentioned school again.

Mom: Do you have school tomorrow?
Me: No, school is out for the summer.
Mom: Okay, good. I wouldn't want you skipping classes.

June 8, 2017

I woke up early to make a really good breakfast....Migas!!! One of my favorites! Dad made it the best, but I make a close second.

Mom: What's this?
Me: I made Migas for breakfast!
Mom: Oh, that's nice. I like it when you make breakfast!

*I make breakfast every morning....

*I was outside mowing for about an hour and had to come in for water.

Mom: Where have you been, and why is your face so red?
Me: I have been outside mowing. I came in for some water.
Mom: I wish I could help you, but I'm just too old.
Me: That's okay mom, you have definitely paid your dues... You just stay in here and relax.
Mom: What dues? Did I forget to pay them?
Me: No Mom, you over-paid!
Mom: Oh okay. Will I get money back?

Mom: You should get someone to mow the yard, you shouldn't have to do that.
Me: It costs too much. I can still mow, so I want to do it. I can't afford to hire someone to do that.
Mom: You need to find a good man to do that for you.

Me: I don't need a man to mow my yard.....I'm independent...

Mom: I just want you to find someone that makes you as happy as your dad made me.

Me: That would be nice, but what you and dad had was one in a million!

Mom: Boy, isn't that the truth! He was such a good man.

Me: I couldn't have asked for better parents.

Mom: That's sweet honey.

Some days are really good....this was one of those days!

June 9, 2017

Mom: Did I drive a car to work today?
Me: No Ma'am.
Mom: I don't even have a car, do I?
Me: No Ma'am.
Mom: Why did I think that I drove to work today?
Me: Maybe you were dreaming?
Mom: Something must be wrong with my mind.

Mom: This cat sure likes jumping in my lap! Is this my cat?
Me: Bonnie is OUR cat, so yes, she is your cat too.
Mom: Well I never know who's who around here. There are so many animals, I don't know which ones are mine any more.
Me: Well, since we both live here, they are all ours.
Mom: I don't think I would have that many if they were mine.

Mom was in the bathroom longer than usual this evening, so I went to check on her.

Me: Mom, are you OKAY?
Mom: Not really.
Me: Can I help?
Mom: Not unless you can make me stop throwing up!

I waited outside the door for about a minute, then she came out....

Mom: Well that was not any fun!

Me: Do you feel bad?
Mom: I'm not sure. I think I ate too much.

Mom eats like a bird, so I know eating too much was not the case! She seemed to be feeling better after that. Hopefully she feels better tomorrow, my roomie surprised me with movie tickets for tomorrow!

June 10, 2017

Don't argue, just go with it no matter how strange it seems.

Mom: Do I need to go back to the school I was at this morning?
Me: We have been home all morning. We only left to get some pool supplies.
Mom: No, I was at school this morning. Do I need to go back?
Me: No mom, you are done for the day.
Mom: Oh, OKAY. Good.

Mom: Were we suppose to pick up someone from the picture show?
Me: No Ma'am.
Mom: Are you sure?
Me: Yes Ma'am.
Mom: Why did I think that?
Me: I'm not sure.
Mom: Maybe I dreamed it.

Mom: I think I need to get back to work.
Me: You are off the rest of the day.
Mom: Are you sure? I sure would hate to get fired for not going back.
Me: No, you don't have to go back until next week.
Mom: Okay, I'll take your word for it.
Me: Would you like a cupcake?
Mom: Yes, that sounds great!

Mom: Did I take my make-up off?

Me: I think so, it looks like you did. You don't have any lipstick on.

Mom: Well, I thought I did. You must think I've lost my mind asking you that.

Me: No, I know you have trouble with your memory. It's okay, that's why I'm here.

Today was a busy day with school and work..... Lots of redirection today when mom was extra confused, at least she was receptive.

June 11, 2017

Some days = no memory!

Me: Are you about ready to leave?
Mom: Where are we going?
Me: We are going to go see Chris today.
Mom: Oh, that's right. I'll go to the bathroom and then I'll be ready.
Me: okay

*10 minutes later mom is still in her room. She is sitting on her bed, just sitting there.

Me: Mom are you okay?
Mom: I can't remember why I came in here. Are we going somewhere?
Me: Yes ma'am. We are going to go see Chris.
Mom: Oh, I didn't know that. When are we leaving?
Me: Now, as soon as you are ready.

Mom: Are we staying here tonight?
Me: We live here.
Mom: I just don't know why I can't get that in my head.
Me: It's okay, mom, I'm here to remind you of whatever you forget.
Mom: Well, thank goodness for that!

*My dog, Red, brings mom a ball to throw. This happens every day, many times a day.

Mom: What am I supposed to do with that?
Me: Throw it.
Mom: In the house?
Me: Yes, just try not to break anything...ha ha ha
Mom: Maybe YOU better throw it!

We visited the kids today and had a nice time.

June 12, 2017

Paranoia is a frequent flyer.

MOM: What are those people doing over there?
Me: They are ordering coffee.
Mom: Are you sure?
Me: Yes ma'am.
Mom: How do you know that?
Me: Because we are at Starbucks and they sell mostly coffee and coffee drinks.
Mom: Oh.

Mom: Where are we going?
Me: We are going to go visit my friend Averi.
Mom: OKAY. How far is it? I feel like we have been driving for hours.
Me: We left the house 20 minutes ago.
Mom: Well that can't be right. You must think I'm just crazy.
Me: No ma'am, I think you are just a little confused sometimes.
Mom: Please don't tell anyone in losing my mind.
Me: Your secret is safe with me.

Averi's little dog Enzo loved mom ♥ ♥

June 13, 2017

Some days can be frustrating.

Mom: Where did that white dog come from?
Me: What white dog?
Mom: That one running around outside.

*I look outside and see no white dog.

Me: I don't see it.
Mom: It must have run away!

*There was never a white dog in the yard

We ate dinner and I gave mom her pills after I cleared the table.

Mom: Don't I have to eat before I take these?
Me: We just finished dinner.
Mom: No we didn't! I think YOU are losing your mind!
Me: What would you like to eat?
Mom: I guess just some cereal.
Me: OKAY, I'll make it for you.

*Mom ate two dinners tonight....

June 14, 2017

Some days you just have to take a breath and let it go.

Mom: What is today?
Me: Today is Wednesday, hair day,
Mom: When do we leave?
Me: We should leave by 11.
Mom: Okay

*We had this same conversation 5 times between 9:30 and 11!

Once we arrived home from the beauty salon…..

Mom: What day do we get our hair done?
Me: We did it today.
Mom: We had our hair done today? Are you sure?
Me: Yes Ma'am, look how beautiful your hair looks!
Mom: I think you are pulling my leg!

*I showed her these pictures and then she believed me!

June 15, 2017

No drastic changes!

Me: Breakfast is ready.
Mom: I didn't know you were in there making breakfast. I could have helped
Me: It's okay, it was quick. I made Migas!
Mom: Do I like Migas?
Me: You liked it the last time I made it.
Mom: okay

I was in the dining room sewing and I could hear mom calling me from the other room. So I went to see what she needed.

Me: Mom, are you okay?
Mom: I'm just looking for Andrea.
*I moved to stand more directly in front of her.
Me: I'm here.
Mom: You look so different! Your hair is so much shorter, I didn't even recognize you!

*Note to self....No drastic changes when caring for someone with Alzheimer's!

Mom: What is today?
Me: Thursday.

Mom: Don't we get our hair done today?
Me: We had our hair one yesterday.
Mom: I sure don't remember that!

*We were there for 3 hours......

June 16, 2017

Sometimes, they revert back to a very distant past.

Mom: Where is everybody?
Me: Who are you looking for?
Mom: All the other people that live here.
Me: Rob is the only other person that lives here with us and he will be home this afternoon.
Mom: No, there are others that live here.
Me: Who are they?
Mom: I don't know, they are YOUR friends, not mine.

*This conversation was on repeat all afternoon …ugh!

Mom: Is this your tea?
Me: Yes, I just poured it.
Mom: I'll take it to the sink.
Me: No, I'm drinking it, I just got it.
Mom: No, this is old, it's been sitting there for hours.

*I put it on the table 5 minutes before she picked it up to dump it out…She does this with drinks and food on a regular basis. Gets frustrating…

I went outside to clean the pool and add chemicals. It was about 1 o'clock in the afternoon.

Mom: Andrea.....Are you out here?
Me: Yes mom, I'm cleaning the pool.
Mom: You need to get back inside, it's getting late.
Me: Mom, it's one o'clock in the afternoon!
Mom: No it's not, it's late.
Me: I'll be in when I'm finished.
Mom: No, come in now.

*I ignored her for about 20 minutes so I could finish cleaning the pool.

She would not allow me to take her picture today....it was a rough day!

June 17, 2017

My roommate, mom and myself went to run errands and then to dinner. That was the entire plan when we left the house.

We arrive to the restaurant......

Mom: Where are we?
Me: We are at the place we are having dinner.
Mom: What about the movie?
Me: We weren't going to a movie, just dinner.
Mom: Well you better tell the others!
Me: There were no....Okay, I will let them know. Let's go eat.
Mom: Well they are going to be mad.

Twenty minutes later in the restaurant....

Mom: Are we leaving soon to meet up with the others.
Me: Mom, there are no others to meet up with.
Mom: They are waiting for us.
Me: They called and said to meet tomorrow instead.
Mom: Are you sure?
Me: Yes ma'am
Mom: Make sure that's true.

We had many similar conversations today....wanting to meet up with friends or "others" from movies to meetings and many in between.

Some days, dogs are my only happy place! I am pet sitting for the sister of one of my dogs, Oaklee!

June 18, 2017

Sometimes you have to tell little white lies.

Mom: We need to go to the cemetery.
Me: OKAY, what for?
Mom: To put flowers on my dad's grave and your dad and my grandfather.
Me: That has all been taken care of.
Mom: Oh, okay good!

Mom: I wish we could do something fun.
Me: We went to dinner last night and that was fun.
Mom: Yeah, I guess. I want to do more fun things.
Me: OKAY, what would you like to do?
Mom: I don't know, go see a movie or something, I don't know.
Me: We could go to painting with a twist or do something like that.
Mom: I don't want to paint.
Me: OKAY. Give it some thought and let me know.
Mom: OKAY.

Me: I'm going outside, why don't you come with me.
Mom: I think I'll stay inside.
Me: It's beautiful outside, come join me.

Mom: I will later.

Me: OKAY. Let me know when you want to come out and I will help you.

Mom: I don't need your help.

June 19, 2017

I was in my room feeding the dogs and mom walks in.

Mom: Where is everybody?
Me: Who are you looking for?
Mom: All the people that live here.
Me: Well you and I are here, Rob is at work and that's it.
Mom: No, there are many more people that live here.
Me: Well where are they?
Mom: I don't know, that's why I am asking you!
Me: Would you like a sweet roll for breakfast?
Mom: That sounds great!

Later in the afternoon.....

Mom: Let's do something.
Me: What would you like to do?
Mom: I don't know, a movie?
Me: Let's look at the previews to find out what's playing.
*We watch several previews.....
Mom: Well I don't want to watch any of those! You couldn't pay me
to go see any of those.
Me: OKAY, what would you like to do then?
Mom: Maybe go back to bed after watching those terrible previews!

This evening......

Mom: Where do I have to be tomorrow?
Me: I don't think you HAVE to be anywhere.
Mom: I thought I had a meeting tomorrow.
Me: Nope, not tomorrow.
Mom: Then when?
Me: Sometime next week.
Mom: You better find out so I don't miss it!

*There is no meeting.....but she won't remember the conversation in 5 minutes....

June 20, 2017

Somedays break my heart.

Mom: I just love this red nail polish. It's too bad I have to give it back!
Me: You are in luck! It's mine and I'm giving it to you!
Mom: No, this belongs to that other lady that lives here.
Me: Well, she told me you could have it.
Mom: Why would she do that?
Me: Because she likes you and thinks you should have it since you like it so much!
Mom: Well, tell her I said Thank you.
Me: I will do that.

*There is no other lady that lives here....

Mom: Is Andrea back yet?
Me: I think so.
Mom: Go tell her to come in here.

*I walk into my room and come out a minute later

Mom: Well, there you are! Where did that other lady go?
Me: She went home.
Mom: Well she sure left abruptly without saying goodbye.
Me: Do you want some ice cream?
Mom: That sounds good, as long as it's chocolate!

Mom: That sure was a nice lady that visited, and her baby was so cute. It was so quiet! What was her name?

Me: That was Averi and her baby Rylee

Mom: Well, you tell them they can visit any time.

Me: It was nice to have company, wasn't it!

Mom: What company?

Me: Averi and her baby.

Mom: Who?

Me: Let's walk outside for a bit.

Mom: OKAY, if you insist!

June 21, 2017

Me: We get to see Chris tomorrow!

Mom: That's nice, when is he coming over?

Me: We are going to go pick him up from a car repair shop. I get to have breakfast and visit with Averi while you and Chris go get breakfast.

Mom: Why don't we all go eat breakfast together?

Me: I thought you might want to spend some time with Chris.

Mom: Okay.

About 3 hours later........

Mom: What time are we picking up Chris from the airport?

Me: We are picking him up from a car repair shop.

Mom: Why did you tell me the airport earlier?

Me: I didn't.

Mom: Where did I get that idea from then?

Me: Maybe you dreamed it...What would you like for dinner?

Mom: I don't know, what are you hungry for?

Later in the evening.......

Mom: What time do we have to leave for the airport in the morning?

Me: We aren't going to the airport, we are going to go pick up Chris from a car repair shop.

Mom: I thought we were going to the Airport!

Me: I wish! It would be nice to go on a plane trip somewhere.

Mom: We should go on a vacation.
Me: Where would you want to go?
Mom: Anywhere.
Me: Fair enough.

June 22, 2017

Thank you Chris, for watching Nana so I could have a day off. It was amazing to have a day off to just relax.

When I got home.....

Mom: How was your trip?
Me: I didn't go on a trip, I hung out with friends and got a massage. I had a gift card for a massage.
Mom: I thought you went on a trip. You are gone for so long I didn't know where you went.
Me: I was only gone for seven hours.
Mom: Oh it was longer than that!
Me: What did you have for lunch?
Mom: I don't remember.
Me: Did you have a hamburger?
Mom: Yes, that's right. I remember now!

It was so wonderful to have a day off! Thank you, Averi, for meeting me for breakfast and helping me with my first live video! Thank you again, Chris, for staying with mom.

June 23, 2017

We went out to run errands and stopped to pick up lunch to take home…..

Mom: We need to get back to the office.
Me: What office?
Mom: The office we work in.
Me: We are retired.
Mom: Well thank goodness! I didn't want to have to go back to work today!
Me: We get to go home now!

Mom: I need to call Andrea to see how she's doing.
Me: Who am I?
Mom: Well, you are going to say you are Andrea, but you don't look like her.
Me: OKAY.
Mom: I think I'm just hungry and confused.
Me: It's okay, at least you figured that out!

Mom: I need to call my sister, Andrea.
Me: Stella Joe was your sister.
Mom: Well Stella Joe and Andrea are both my sisters.
Me: Mom, I'm Andrea, your daughter.
Mom: I know, but I have another Andrea
Me: OKAY….Are you ready for bed?
Mom: I think so. I think I'm going to go lay down.

117

Me: I think that's a great idea, good night.

I was working on some things on my computer, trying to get some paperwork done. Mom came back into the kitchen nook 3 times before finally going to bed. It's almost impossible to get things done when she is up, or interrupting me every 5 minutes, only to ask the same question for the fifteenth time!

June 24, 2017

*Sometimes mom has conversations with the dogs. I wasn't going to post them, but it's just too funny. Those of you who really know me, know how I feel about my furry children. My 4 year old lab mix loves to get pets from mom and sometimes gets a little pushy.... The following conversation happens at least twice a day!

Mom: Okay, Mia, I love you too.

*Mia pushes her nose under mom's arm to get her to pet her.

Mom: Mia, how am I supposed to read the paper if you keep doing that?

*Mia talks back, under protest.

Mom: Well, alright, I'll pet you some more.

Me: How about we go out to dinner tonight, I don't feel like cooking.
Mom: Well, I sure as hell am NOT cooking!
Me: OKAY, let's go out.
Mom: What about everyone else?
Me: Who?
Mom: All the others that go out to eat with us.
Me: It's just you and I tonight.
Mom: Well, you better call everyone to let them know.
Me: Let them know......Okay, mom I will let them know.

Mom: Who's driving us?

Me: I thought I would drive.

Mom: Do you know how?

Me: *Shaking my head.... Yes mom, I think I can handle it.

Mom: I need more facial cleanser.

Me: OKAY, let me see the bottle.

Mom: What in the world for?

Me: So I can take a picture of it, so I know what to buy next time we are at HEB.

Mom: That's just silly. It will take longer to get the film developed than just taking the jar with us!

June 25, 2017

Every day is a new day!

Mom: What is today?
Me: Sunday.

*Five minutes later.....

Mom: What is today?
Me: Sunday

*This conversation went on for over an hour until we left to go visit Chris.

Later in the evening.....

Mom: Where is everyone?
Me: It's just you and me tonight.
Mom: Well, where did everyone go.
Me: I'm not sure. It's just you and me tonight. Would you like some ice-cream?
Mom: Yes, that sounds good!

We visited the kids today and it was fantastic!!! ❤ ❤ ❤ ❤ ❤ ❤

June 26, 2017

I just love her honest answers!

Mom: When do we go get our hair done?
Me: Wednesday.
Mom: Do I need to wash my hair before we go?
Me: No, they do that for you when you get there.
Mom: I know I keep asking you this, I just can't remember anything!
Me: That's okay, mom, that's why I'm here.

Mom: Where do we live?
Me: We live here, in this house, in Georgetown.
Mom: Georgetown?
Me: Yes Ma'am.
Mom: Well, when did we move here?
Me: Two years ago.
Mom: Are you sure about that?
Me: Yes Ma'am. Would you like some iced tea?
Mom: That sounds good.

Mom: Where are we going?
Me: We need to run a few errands this morning.
Mom: Oh. Where are we coming from?
Me: We just left the house. Now we are headed to the Post Office.
Mom: What are you doing at the post office?
Me: I have a few things to mail.

Mom: Where are we going after that?
Me: Where would you like to go?
Mom: On a cruise.
Me: Well, we will have to wait a bit on that...

*Sometimes mom says the funniest things!

June 27, 2017

Some days are tough, others tougher!

Me: Are you ready to go?
Mom: Where are we going?
Me: To visit Averi and have breakfast with her.
Mom: Oh, that's right, I forgot. Are we going Christmas shopping after that?
Me: I think it's a little early for that.
Mom: When is Christmas?
Me: Christmas is in December, which is 6 months away.
Mom: I guess we should wait awhile for Christmas shopping.

Mom: Can you drive my car back home?
Me: We are in my car.
Mom: Well, where is my car?
Me: You sold your car 2 years ago.
Mom: I don't remember that, are you sure?
Me: Yes ma'am.
Mom: Huh, I don't remember that. You need to call everyone in Shiner to let them know we will be late.
Me: OKAY, I did that. Everyone knows we will be late.
Mom: OKAY.

Today was one of the toughest days. Mom wasn't feeling well and spent a couple of hours in the bathroom. When she came out, she was weak and could barely walk. Averi and I were able to get her situated and back in the car long enough to get her home. For the first time, I had to actually shower mom, she couldn't help at all. She was too weak to stand on her own. I had to use the wheelchair to get her to bed after her shower and she went to sleep within 5 minutes. Alzheimer's really sucks! I am not sharing this for sympathy, I am sharing to help raise awareness. Being a full time caregiver for a parent is NOT easy and not pretty, but it sure is rewarding. I know I am giving mom the best care she can receive….until the day comes that I am no longer capable of doing so.

I want to thank Averi for all the help today, being my friend and having the patience of a saint! I had a good time today, despite the "crappy" ending!

June 28, 2017

Who's on first!??

Mom: When do we get our hair done?
Me: Today at noon.
Mom: Well why didn't you tell me!!! I have to get ready!!!
Me: Mom, it's only 8:30, I think you have time.
Mom: You better go get dressed and ready.
Me: I will. We aren't leaving until 11:00.
Mom: How much time do I have to get ready?
Me: Two and a half hours.
Mom: I better get started!

Mom: When do we go pick up my car?
Me: You don't have a car any more.
Mom: Well how do I get around?
Me: I drive you.
Mom: How will I get home?
Me: I will take you.
Mom: You can't keep driving me around
Me: I have been for 3 years......
Mom: Are you sure about that?
Me: Yes Ma'am.

We had just arrived back home from getting our hair done......5 minutes later......

Mom: When do we get our hair done?
Me: We did that today..
Mom: When?
Me: At noon.
Mom: It's just 1:30, how could we have done that at noon?
Me: We just got home from the shop.
Mom: What shop?
Me: The beauty shop.
Mom: What did we do there?
Me: You had your hair done.
Mom: When?
Me: Just an hour ago.
Mom: You ramble too much.

I feel like I'm in the "Who's on First" skit!!!!! Calgon....take me away....Pleeeease!

Later this afternoon.......

Mom: I think I am going to call Andrea, my daughter.
Me: Mom, I am your daughter.
Mom: You are my pretend daughter, not my real daughter. She lives in Houston.
Me: I am Andrea, your daughter. You are my Mom, Pat. Harry was my dad and your husband.

*Mom walked off mumbling something I couldn't understand. She returned to the dining room where I was working and proceeded to pull out pictures of me when I was in my 20's or 30's....

Mom: See, THIS is my daughter and that's definitely NOT you! So quit telling lies saying you are my daughter. You are going to get into a lot of trouble telling people that!

Me: OKAY.
Mom: Are you going to stop this?

*I just walked away…..starting to feel a little defeated and down.

June 29, 2017

Sometimes mom can be hurtful!

Mom: Good morning!

Me: Good Morning! How are you feeling?

Mom: Fine. Why would you ask that?

Me: You were extra confused yesterday. Do you remember who I am?

Mom: You are the one taking care of me.

Me: That's right and I am also your daughter.

Mom: Are we starting in on that already? It's too early for that!

Mom: What time is Chris picking me up?

Me: I don't think Chris is coming today.

Mom: He said he was taking me home today.

Me: Maybe he will be here later.

Mom: I better call him.

Me: He's at work right now, let's wait awhile.

Mom: Where am I sleeping tonight?

Me: In your room. Would you like me to show you?

Mom: Well, yes, I don't know where anything is in this house!

*I show mom her room.....the same room she has had for 2 years!

Mom: Where will you sleep?
Me: In my room.
Mom: Where is your room?

*I showed her my room.

Mom: Who lives here?
Me: We do. We have lived here for 2 years.
Mom: Maybe you have, but I haven't.

Her memory seems to be getting progressively worse. It's heartbreaking to watch such a rapid decline! Alzheimer's really sucks! I know I have said that – a lot, but it really does!

June 30, 2017

Technology can be very confusing and frustrating.

Mom: Why is my phone blinking red?
Me: It needs to be charged. Would you like me to plug it in for you?
Mom: OKAY.
Me: I am plugging it in her on the counter.

*Five minutes later.....

Mom: I can't find my phone anywhere!
Me: I just plugged it in to charge.
Mom: Where?
Me: On the counter.
Mom: It should be finished by now.
Me: We just plugged it in, so let's leave it over night to charge.
Mom: Oh Alright!

Mom: Where is everybody?
Me: Who are you lookaying for?
Mom: All the others that live here.
Me: You and I and Rob are the only people that live here.
Mom: I don't believe you.

Mom: Where did Andrea go?

Me: Who are you looking for?

Mom: Andrea, my daughter. She was here earlier.

Me: Mom, I'm here.

Mom: No, you are mistaken, you are not Andrea.

I should just say, "I don't know where she is" or "She went home", but I just can't bring myself to do it! I feel the need to continue to remind her I am her daughter and I am STILL here!

July 1, 2017

The frustration of confusion!

I went to bed early because I overheated. I told mom good night and went to bed about 9:00... I wake up to the door flying open and the light coming on.....

Mom: It's time to get up.
Me: No, mom, it's 10:00 at night, go to bed.
Mom: I was wondering why it was so dark. Good night.

Ugh.........I was sound asleep!!!

I'm exhausted...I will post more tomorrow..... to be continued..

July 2, 2017

In time, she will forget!

Mom: Is today Wednesday?
Me: No, today is Sunday.
Mom: Are you sure? It feels more like Wednesday.
Me: I'm sure...today is Sunday.

Mom: It's dad picking us up today?
Me: I don't think so.
Mom: Well, you better find out. He will be upset if we aren't ready when he gets here.
Me: I'll call him.

* Five minutes later she didn't remember the conversation.

July 3, 2017

Mom: What are we doing here?
Me: I am delivering the small blankets I made to Terri.
Mom: Can I just wait in the car?
Me: Sure, I will be right back.
Mom: OKAY

*I was gone 5 minutes or less...

Mom: I thought you were taking in some blankets or something.
Me: I did. I took the blankets inside.
Mom: I didn't see you carrying anything in.
Me: Yes ma'am, I sure did.
Mom: Well, I didn't see you take anything in.

Mom: I am really mixed up.
Me: What are you mixed up about?
Mom: Do I live here?
Me: Yes Ma'am, we both live here.
Mom: Where is my room?
Me: Back over that way.
Mom: Do I have a bathroom?
Me: Yes Ma'am, it's by your bedroom.
Mom: Why am I so mixed up?
Me: You have Alzheimer's.
Mom: Oh, really?

Mom: Who was that young lady with the baby?
Me: That is my friend Averi and her baby Rylee.
Mom: How do you know her.
Me: We graduated from Southwestern together.
Mom: Do I have to go to school tomorrow?
Me: No, we are on holiday.
Mom: OKAY good.

Today my dad would have been 86 years old. I miss him every day.

Mom got a real kick out of Snapchat! She was amazed it could put bunny ears on us in the picture....she can be so easily amused!

July 4, 2017

Hair today…gone tomorrow!

Mom: When is hair day?
Me: Tomorrow.
Mom: What is today?
Me: Tuesday.
Mom: Is tomorrow Saturday?
Me: Tomorrow is Wednesday.
Mom: I just can't seem to remember anything anymore.
Me: It's OKAY mom, that's why I'm here.

Mom: Where is that lady that cooks for us?
Me: I cook for us.
Mom: I thought some other lady cooked for us.
Me: I am the lady that cooks, cleans, does laundry and takes care of everything here.
Mom: That's a big job for one person.
Me: Tell me about it!
Mom: Well, you do a good job.

Mom didn't remember the pictures we took yesterday, so I showed her the filters on Snapchat again and she was just as tickled today as she was yesterday…. I told her to pick one to post and she liked these two, so I am posting them both at her request…

July 5, 2017

*Plans can change at the drop of a hat! Always
be prepared for plan B, or C or...*

We met my friend Averi for breakfast this morning and had a good
visit. About 30 minutes after we arrived......

Mom: Are we leaving soon or are we staying here all day? People may
want to sit down and we are just taking up space.
Me: Mom, there are 10 tables that are empty, I am sure if someone
wants to sit, there are plenty of places for them to do so.
Mom: Well we should go soon anyway.
Me: It's nice to have a change of scenery. Let's just stay awhile longer.
Mom: I don't want to.
Me: OKAY. We will go then.

Mom: Where did I put my suitcase?
Me: It's probably in your room, under your bed or next to your
dresser. Why?
Mom: Well if we are staying, I will need to unpack it.
Me: I think you already unpacked it.
Mom: I doubt it. I didn't know if we were staying here or going back.
Me: Mom, we live here.
Mom: No, I don't. Maybe you live here but I live in Houston.
Me: OKAY, mom.

Mom: What time do we have to get up for work in the morning?

Me: We don't have to get up early tomorrow.

Mom: Don't we have to get up for work? I don't want to be late!

Me: We won't be late. You can sleep in tomorrow. We are off tomorrow.

Mom: Is tomorrow Saturday?

Me: No…..Yes, it is….Tomorrow is Saturday!

Mom actually remembered the snap chat filters today and wanted to do it again. This time I used the flowers…She kept asking me if that was really on her head. That must really mess with her mind…. It's in the picture but not really on her head…how did it get there in the picture….

July 6, 2017

Sometimes it's the small pleasures that mean so much!

Mom: What kind of flowers are we?
Me: We are lions!
Mom: Well that's silly... what else can we do?
Me: How about some cool sunglasses?
Mom: Oh my goodness, that's funny!

Mom was pretty quiet today. Most of what she said didn't make much sense. She did seem to enjoy snapchat again today!

July 7, 2017

We were watching Family feud and the question was....Name a big city in Texas....One of the contestants said "Little Boot"......

Mom: What in the world was that lady thinking...She must be a Yankee!
Me: *Laughing so hard I'm in tears....* Why would you think she is a Yankee?
Mom: Because everyone knows that's not a big city!
Mom: Where are we going to dinner?
Me: Rob is taking us out to Scott's Oyster Bar for dinner.
Mom: Well, that sure is nice of him!
Me: It sure is!

*3 minutes later...

Mom: What are we doing for dinner tonight?
Me: Rob is taking to out to dinner.
Mom: What time?
Me: In about an hour.
Mom: That early?
Me: It's already after 5
Mom: Oh okay.

*a few minutes later.

Mom: Where did Andrea go? She is taking me to dinner.

*Shaking my head…..

We did a couple snapchat filters today and she was shocked by the one that gave me a big mouth….

July 8, 2017

I had a booth at the Georgetown Market Days and had a bit of heat exhaustion and fell asleep earlier than usual!

Chris was kind enough to entertain mom...AKA Nana.... all day, so I was able to work on my Color Street business!

We got home and ate...we both took showers and sat in the living room for a little while.....

Mom: Are we staying here tonight?
Me: Yes ma'am...we are at home...
Mom: What?
Me: Yes ma'am, we are staying here tonight.

Before we went home, I stopped to pick up some dinner so I didn't have to cook.... I found the Goth filter on Snapchat.... She took one look at this picture and said....Eewww....what's THAT?!?!?! I haven't laughed that hard in a long time!

July 9, 2017

Mom: What are we doing today?
Me: I have to run to Hutto, want to come?
Mom: Yes, I need to get dressed.
Me: OKAY

*I wait about 5 minutes and as I am about to go check on mom, she comes out of her room...still in her PJ's

Mom: I can't remember what I came in here to do.
Me: We have to go run an errand, you were getting dressed.
Mom: Oh, I think I'll just stay here.
Me: I don't want to drive by myself, please come with me.
Mom: Oh, alright, I'll get dressed.

*I can't leave her alone unless it's just a few minutes, so this is my way of trying to get her to go with me. Sometimes it works, sometimes it doesn't....I am really glad it worked today!

Mom: It looks like it could storm out there!
Me: Yes, it does! That loud noise was thunder.
Mom: It was?
Me: Yes ma'am!
Mom: Well, we better get home before it does!
Me: Well, it's a good thing we ARE home!
Mom: Well, I guess that's true.

Mom: Where do I live?
Me: You live here with me.
Mom: And you are....
Me: Andrea, your daughter.
Mom: Are you sure about that? You sure don't look like her!

I know I keep posting Snapchat pictures, but they really make me laugh and more important, they make MOM laugh! We all need to remember to laugh....life is too short!

When we did the picture with the bows and white sunglasses, mom said....I think I had a bow like that when I was a girl! Ha ha ha ha ha!

July 10, 2017

Today was a rough day. I had an appointment at a memory care facility. I feel like mom would be more active in a place better equipped to handle her situation. The place I visited was so beautiful and everyone there was so nice and helpful. While I was talking to Kelly, I felt like we were on the exact same page! I know this won't happen within the next month, but I feel like it's the right thing to do, especially for mom. I feel like she and I are disconnected much of the time, even when we are in the same room. I try to interact with her and she just seems more and more lost. I truly hope I am doing the right thing. Some of the ladies at the facility kept mom busy while I visited with Kelly. When we were reunited.....

Mom: There you are! I was wondering where you went.
Me: I'm right here.

Once we got in the car......

Mom: I thought you had just dropped me off to leave me there!
Me: No, we were just visiting. What did you think? They sure do a lot of activities there! Did you see all the puzzles and games they had out?
Mom: Oh yeah, sure. That's just to make you think they do things all day.
Me: Well, they do have activities all throughout the day to keep you busy. Don't you get tired of being around just me all the time?
Mom: No, I sure don't, but I bet you get tired of being around me all of the time!

Me: No, mom, I enjoy your company.

Later in the afternoon.......

Mom: Are you staying here tonight?
Me: Yes ma'am.
Mom: OK, good. I don't want to be left alone after the day I've had!
Me: OK
Mom: Do I have a room here?
Me: Yes ma'am, you sure do.
Mom: Can you tell me where it is?
Me: Yes, it's right around the corner.
Mom: Are you sure that's my room? I don't want to walk in on someone if that's not my room.
Me: I am sure that is your room. Let's go check it out.
Mom: Well, that all looks like my stuff, so I guess this is my room.

We had a very cute visitor today! It was great to see you, Averi! Thank you for bringing Rylee to visit!

July 11, 2017

Today was a little less stressful than yesterday where mom's confusion is concerned. She's still confused, just not like yesterday. The only thing I can compare yesterday to, was like a little kid panic-stricken because they can't find their parent. The change in the dynamic of our relationship is sometimes frightening. Mom has always been so independent and strong, so to see this side of her is just, well, strange to say the least. This is part of why I am terrified to let her live at a facility, even though I feel in my heart, it's the right thing. I just don't want her to remember me as her daughter that abandoned her… even though I would visit all the time. I still have to figure out the financials, which has been a challenge. For those of you that do not have long term care insurance, look into it! If you don't have it and find yourself needing it…..well, it's so much more difficult to get it when you really need it!

Mom: I think my nail polish is wearing off.
Me: well, let's see. Yup, it's definitely time to redo it!
Mom: Well, can you do it?
Me: Can I put the Color Street nail polish strips on you?
Mom: Sure, as long as they are red!
Me: Ok. How about the Moulin Rouge one.
Mom: That's pretty. Ok.

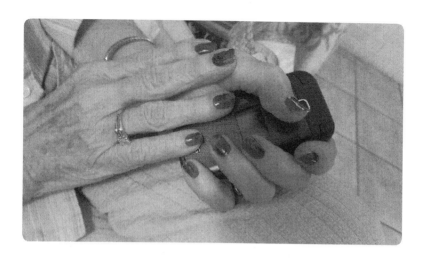

I told mom she could be a hand model....she laughed ☺

Mom: Are we going back tonight?
Me: Back to where?
Mom: Back to where we came from.
Me: Where did we come from?
Mom: You know, I'm not sure!
Me: Ok, let me know when you figure it out.
Mom: Ok

Mom: What on earth are we watching?
Me: It's a dancing competition called World of Dance.
Mom: They look crazy!
Me: Dancing is a little different than when you were young.
Mom: Boy, I would say so! We didn't throw each other around!
Me: Ha ha ha ha

July 12, 2017

Humor me!

I was out in the garage moving a few things around. Mom was in the living room. I told her I was going into the garage to rearrange a few things. I was in the garage less than 5 minutes before she came out into the garage.

Mom: Well, there you are! I have been looking everywhere for you!
Me: Here I am!
Mom: I've just been sitting in there bored to tears! I just don't know what to do with myself!
Me: Be careful, I'll put you to work!
Mom: Well, I'm going back inside. It's too hot for you to be out here.
Me: I will be in in a bit.

Mom: Do we get our hair done today?
Me: We sure did get our hair done today.

Yes, I realize she asked me if we were getting our hair done, but since we already had, I acted like she just made a statement that we had already had our hair done. We had only been home an hour! She had a perm and I cut my hair into a pixy!

Me: Mom, can I make you a sandwich for lunch?

Mom: I can do it, you do everything around here, I can at least make my own sandwich. You take really good care of me, you know that?
Me: Well, thank you mom!

Some days are good. It is particularly rewarding when she recognizes that I take care of her. Makes it even harder to make a decision to find mom a place away from home and me.

July 13, 2017

Keep It Simple!

I know I keep going back and forth on keeping mom at home or finding a facility that she might be happier in, than with me in my home. In my heart, I feel like she is happy most of the time and I feel like this is what my dad would want me to do. Those of you who know me, KNOW I am a daddy's girl through and through! I feel like I would worry about her all the time if she was not with me. I've been at this for 3 years and I feel like it has made us closer. I believe there is a happy medium, so I have decided to look more into a place I can take her a few days a week that encourage senior activities. I feel this will give me a little free time to get out and do things I enjoy and give mom some mental stimulation with people she can better relate to. Maybe this isn't the answer for everyone in this situation, but I feel it is the best solution for mom and I.

I did some of moms' laundry today and since she likes a "job" I asked if she wanted to hang up her clean clothes…

Mom: Oh my goodness, these are beautiful!
Me: They are yours, mom.
Mom: Oh, are you sure? They are so colorful and beautiful! Where did you get them?
Me: They were in the hamper in the laundry room. They are your clothes.

Mom: Well, I sure do have good taste!
Me: Yes, mom, you sure do!

Me: Mom, would you like a glass of wine with dinner?
Mom: Well, yes, that would be very nice!
Me: What kind would you like, red or white?
Mom: Well, honey, that's doesn't matter. I've never met a glass of wine I didn't like!
Me: Well, ok...white it is!

Mom: Can we do those silly pictures, the ones with the bunny ears and stuff?
Me: Sure. We can look at Snapchat.
Mom: That one is funny...are those brown ears?
Me: Yes, those are brown ears.

July 14, 2017

Mom: Can I put these dirty dishes in the oven?
Me: You mean the dish washer?
Mom: Isn't that what I said?
Me: Yes ma'am, you sure can, the dishes in the dish washer are dirty.

We have this conversation at least 10 times a day.

Mom: Did you feed all the animals?
Me: Yes ma'am, I sure did!
Mom: Even the birds?
Me: Sure, even the birds.

We don't have any birds!

Mom: Can I go get ready for bed?
Me: Sure, whenever you are ready.
Mom: Is my room back there?
Me: Yes ma'am, it sure is.
Mom: Can you show me? Nothing over there looks familiar.
Me: Sure, mom, right this way.

She was a little more confused today. I noticed she didn't drink but one cup of coffee today…

July 15, 2017

Today was a long, but very successful day! Thanks, Averi, for hanging in there with me today! Thank you to Rob, my roommate for keeping an eye on my mom today so I could try to make a little money!

When I returned from a long hot afternoon of working...

Mom: Well hello! I didn't expect you back until next week!
Me: Well, I came home early!
Mom: What a nice surprise! You didn't have to stay longer?
Me: No, we finished the job!
Mom: Well, that's great! I'm glad you are home.

I wasn't going to be gone long. I left really early (way before she even got up) and was home by 4 this afternoon. I left her a note that I would be back around 4.

Mom and I were in the car and it started to rain a little...

Mom: What are all those little bugs flying off the windshield?
Me: Those are raindrops that are rolling off the windshield. There is a coating that helps the raindrops not stick to the windshield so much,
Mom: I think you are pulling my leg!
Me: Then they must be little bugs.
Mom: Well, that's what I thought!

She makes me laugh so hard sometimes!

July 16, 2017

Sometimes you just need to lock the bathroom door!

Me: Mom, I'm going to go take a shower. I will be out in a few minutes.
Mom: Okay.

Less than 5 minutes later, mom knocks on the bathroom door, then just walks in!

Me: Mom, I'm in the shower. I'll be out in a little while. Mom: Okay, I didn't know where you were. You didn't tell me.

Sometimes boundaries are nonexistent.

Mom loved the wolf snapchat filter! Sometimes it's the only way I can amuse her!

July 17, 2017

Sometimes you have to laugh to keep from crying!

Mom was unusually quiet today. Some days are just like that. Some days she just seems to zone out, so I will take her for a walk down the driveway to stimulate her mind some. I believe getting her into a program this week will help her with mental stimulation.

Me: Let's go for a short walk down the driveway.
Mom: Well, okay, I can do that.
Me: Let's get your walker.
Mom: That's not mine.
Me: Yes, this is your walker. Remember the pretty red poppy bag I made to tie on it so you can put your purse in it?
Mom: I remember that, but I don't think that's my walker. I think that belongs to the other lady that lives here.
Me: What other lady?
Mom: I don't know…some other lady.
Me: Okay. Well let's take it out there anyway.
Mom: Okay, but I don't want her yelling at me if she finds out I used it.
Me: I will make sure she never knows.

Mom: Can we take a funny picture today?
Me: Yes ma'am, we sure can!

Mom really loves the snap chat filters, a lot!

July 18, 2017

Remember to take time to socialize with friends, even if you have to take your loved one with Alzheimer's with you!

Mom: When do we get our hair done?
Me: Tomorrow at noon.
Mom: What is today?
Me: Tuesday.
Mom: What day do we get our hair done?
Me: Wednesday at noon.

We left late in the afternoon to meet Averi for a coffee and later we met Kelly for dinnner!

While we were waiting for Averi at Cianfrani, I noticed mom was figeting with her straw that was in her tea.

Me: What are you doing, mom?
Mom: I'm trying to get the straw back in the package.
Me: Don't you need it for your tea?
Mom: Well, I was just trying to get it back in the package so I can use it later.
Me: It's a disposable straw, you can get another one later. Use this one for now.
Mom: Well, what if I don't want to.
Me: Averi is here!

Later at dinner...

Kelly: Ms Pat, you should get a streak of color in your hair like Andrea!
Mom: Oh yeah, right! People would think I was crazy. They would say what a ticky tacky old lady!
Me: Do you think people say I'm ticky tacky with my colorful hair?
Mom: No, you aren't old!
Kelly and I got a really good laugh with that!

July 19, 2017

Some days may feel like you have entered the twilight zone!

Mom and I went to get our hair done today at noon. Mom gets her hair done every Wednesday at noon, every week.

2:30 in the afternoon after we ate lunch. I had the TV on for mom to watch one of her favorite game shows.

Mom: Don't we go get our hair done today?
Me: Yes ma'am, we had it done at noon today.
Mom: What time do you have?
Me: It's 2:30.
Mom: Well I guess we missed my appointment.
Me: No we didn't, you had your air done at noon.

Later…

Mom: I think I'll take a ciggarette break.
Me: Oh? When did you start smoking?
Mom: I just thought I would try it.
Me: How about we go take a walk down the driveway instead.
Mom: Well, okay, that would be nice.

Mom has never been a smoker, so I have no idea were that came from!

Mom: Show me that picture thing again.

Me: Snapchat?
Mom: I don't know what you call it!
Me: How about a banana head?
Mom: Well that's just silly! (As she giggled!)

July 20, 2017

Me: Good morning, Mom!

Mom: Good morning.

Me: How are you this morning?

Mom: I have no idea, it too early to tell.

Me: I am going to go get dressed. We are going to Killeen this morning.

Mom: What on earth for?

Me: We are going to do an event there next month, so we are going to go check it out first before we decide to commit to it.

Mom: That's a long drive, isn't it?

Me: Not really...about an hour.

Mom: Oh, no, it's farther than that! You have to drive past Austin and that is at least a couple of hours.

Me: Where are we driving from?

Mom: Houston, where else would we be driving from?

We live in Georgetown...Not Houston!

Mom: Where are we staying tonight?

Me: Where do you think we are staying?

Mom: I guess here?

Me: That's right. Do you know why we are staying here?

Mom: I think you live here.

Me: Yes, ma'am, we both live here.

Mom: That's right. Why can't I remember that?

I wanted to take a regular picture tonight, but mom wouldn't have it!
So…it's back to Snapchat!

July 22, 2017

Me: Mom, where is your walker?
Mom: I don't know, where is your walker?
Me: I don't have one.
Mom: Well, neither do I!

I went into her room, found her walker and brought it to her!

Mom: Did the paper get here yet?
Me: I'm sure it's in the driveway.
Mom: I guess I will go out and get it.
Me: Okay.
Mom: Will you come with me?
Me: Sure!

Sometimes that is the most exercise she gets that day, so I always make her get the paper. It's very difficult to get her to do things. That's why I think taking her to a Senior care place once or twice a week would be good for her! She will listen to other people much more than she will listen to me!

July 23, 2017

Sometimes they revert!

I don't think mom will ever want to take a normal picture. She asks me almost every night, if we can take pictures with that funny camera.

Mom: Where is my room? I just can't seem to remember.
Me: It's that way, at the end of the hall.
Mom: I just can't seem to remember anything these days.
Me: It's okay, mom. I will remind you when you forget.
Mom: Thank goodness you are here to remind me!
Mom: Can we take more funny pictures?
Me: Yes, we can!

And, YES, that is mom sticking out her tongue! I feel like I have a teenager sometimes.

July 24, 2017

Remember: Their reality isn't your reality, just go with it.

Mom: Did we have somewhere to be tonight?
Me: I don't think so.
Mom: I thought we were scheduled to be somewhere.
Me: Chris is coming over today to pick up the puppies.
Mom: Well that will be good to see him!
Me: Yes it will.

Mom: Do I need to write my hours down?
Me: Hours for…?
Mom: Working.
Me: I don't think we need to do that.
Mom: Well I haven't been but I didn't know if I should or not.
Me: I think we are ok.
Mom: So we don't have to write our hours down?
Me: No ma'am.
Mom: Okay

One of the things mom is obsessed with is the dish washer. This has been an ongoing thing for the past 2+ years. She will ask me at least 10 times a day if the dishes in the dish washer are dirty or clean. I made a sign to put on the dishwasher "Dishes are dirty" in hopes she would stop asking all the time and that worked for about a month. Now she is back at it! I think I will try making a sign that looks different, maybe a different font and color. Maybe that will help. I will let you know in a few weeks.

July 25, 2017

Find a support network, it helps make you feel less alone.

Mom: Where are we going?
Me: We are going to go meet Kelly for dinner.
Mom: Why?
Me: To visit and hang out. She is bring us some wonderful farm fresh eggs!
Mom: That's nice.

Mom: Where is your bedroom?
Me: It's behind where we are sitting.
Mom: My room is on the other side of the house, right?
Me: Yes ma'am.
Mom: I wish our rooms weren't so far apart.
Me: It's ok, it's just at night.
Mom: Maybe we can share your room.
Me: We can talk about that tomorrow.
Mom: Okay

Today, I went to an Alzheimer's support group, for the first time ever! It was really nice to be surrounded by people that are going through the same things I am going through. Hearing from others made me feel less alone. This was the first time I have been surrounded by people who could relate to my situation, my heartbreak and the everyday struggles.

If you are in a similar situation or know someone who is, I highly recommend getting into a support group, being there really made me feel better and stronger!

July 26, 2017

Talk to your Dr. about med adjustments when things seem off.

Some days are just tougher than others. I have noticed mom slowing down more and more and her temper becoming quicker. I spent some time on the phone today with some publishers, trying to figure out how I can get my work published. Mom did not like me being on the phone, which has become more and more of an issue. Not only am I, at her mercy to leave the house, phone calls are the next privilege I will have to give up.

Mom: Who are you talking to?
Me: I'll be finished in a few minutes.
Mom: Get off that phone. It better not be long distance!
Me: No, mom, it's not long distance.
Mom: You need to come in here and get your chores done.

Apparently I have a list of chores I need to do! I did not get off the phone right away, so mom came back into my room and we had the same conversation all over again!

Mom: What are you doing?
Me: I am working on the computer.
Mom: Well you need to get off of there and help me with some things.
Me: Okay, what do you need help with?
Mom: You need to come in here.

Mom led me into her room and when we got there she asked me why I was following her! Seriously!?!

I would love everyone to help me raise awareness about Alzheimer's disease and its effects on everyone. Those with Alzheimer's disease don't have a voice. Help me, help other caregivers and family members. If you found any value in my book, please share this information.

July 27, 2017

Good night.…Good night.…

Mom: Do we have anything sweet?
Me: Yes ma'am, we have some candy.
Mom: Can you take all the calories out of it?
Me: Sure, mom, I can do that. Ha ha ha.

Mom went to bed, said good night to me and went to her room. I went to my room and 30 minutes later she came waltzing into my room scaring the crap out of me!

Mom: I forgot to say good night to everyone.
Me: We said good night.
Mom: Well, there's nothing wrong with me! Where did everyone else go?
Me: Who are you referring to?
Mom: I don't know, the other people that live here.
Me: It's just you and I, mom.
Mom: Well, I guess I will go to bed. Should I turn off the lights?
Me: I'll take care of the lights. Good night.
Mom: Good night.

July 28, 2017

Sometimes you just need a puppy!

It has been a very busy past few days!

Mom: Where did this puppy come from? Did one of these have a baby?
Me: No. We are baby/pet sitting for the weekend.
Mom: Sure is a cute puppy!
Me: Do you want to hold her?
Mom: Sure.

10 minutes later...

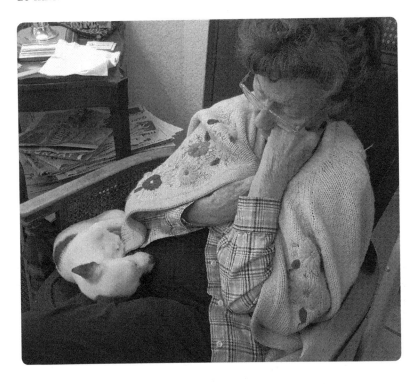

July 29, 2017

I'll say it again…Sometimes you just need a puppy!

Mom: Why are you up so early?
Me: I just wanted to get an early start to get some things done. I need to go to the shelter today, will you come with me?
Mom: I guess so. You aren't getting another dog, are you?
Me: No, mom, we are not getting another dog.
Mom: You aren't getting another cat, are you?
Me: No mom, we are not getting another cat.
Mom: Well, what are you getting at the shelter?
Me: I am dropping off some artwork.
Mom: Oh, okay!

Later the same day, after visiting the shelter…

Mom: NOW where are we going?
Me: I just need to get some dog and cat food.
Mom: I thought you didn't get any more pets at the shelter.
Me: I didn't, I need food for our existing fur babies.
Mom: What is a fur baby?
Me: Our pets…ha ha ha

I am pet sitting for a 7 week old puppy and I took her everywhere with us! I made a little sling like carrier I could keep her in while we ran errands. I had no idea it was so therapeutic to hold a puppy all day as you did errands. I have never been so relaxed and calm while running errands!

The best part was how she rode in the car!

July 30, 2017

*Remember, their reality is not always the
same as yours! Adapt and conform!*

Mom: Did you drop off that paperwork?
Me: What paperwork?
Mom: The paperwork we needed to send to the school for classes.
Me: I sure did!

There is no paperwork for school.

Mom: Are we keeping the puppy?
Me: No, we are just pet sitting for the weekend.
Mom: That's too bad, she sure is sweet.
Me: Yes ma'am, she is.
Mom: Maybe we can just keep her.
Me: She has already been adopted.
Mom: Well, that's too bad.

Mom: Where are we going tonight?
Me: I don't think we are going anywhere, why?
Mom: I think I had a date tonight.
Me: Oh! Who do you have a date with?
Mom: I don't remember.
Me: That's okay, just let me know when you remember.

Going along with her thoughts and present memories is the only way to keep harmony and peace. Arguing only makes things harder for her and she, in turn, makes things harder on me. This memory of a date could have been with my dad or could have gone back even farther, so making a suggestion of someone in particular could have agitated her. Asking her to let me know when she remembers gives her time to reset and possibly come back to a more current time.

July 31, 2017

Animals are therapeutic and highly recommended!

Today, our little furry visitor, Nebula went back to her foster family. We will really miss her around here. I received a text that they had arrived and told mom I was taking her out to them. When I came back inside, mom met me in the garage and asked where Nebula was. I told her the people fostering her picked her up and mom had the saddest look on her face and said, I didn't get to say goodbye! That is the most emotion I have seen from her in years! So, of course I ran back outside to catch Jennifer and she was, thankfully, still in the driveway! So I asked her if mom could say good bye to Nebula and of course handed her to me. I took Nebula to mom and this was the conversation that still has me laughing!

Mom: Now you be a good girl. If you are bad, maybe they will bring you back. On second thought, be really bad!

Mom gave her a kiss on the head and turned around and I swear that woman was teary eyed!

Mom: I sure wish that little dog could have stayed.
Me: Me too! You know we have 5 dogs already.
Mom: I know, but we all liked her so much, even the big dogs liked her!
Me: I know.
Mom: None of the other dogs can sit in my lap.

Me: Mom, you aren't helping! I loved her too, but she is already adopted to another family. She will have 3 children to play with in a loving home really soon. Her foster family loves her very much too. She is in good hands.

Mom: If you say so.

I had no idea mom became so attached. The cats spend a bit of time in her lap, but the puppy was in her lap more. She would fall asleep with Nebula in her lap, it was so cute and sweet!

Mom spent the next two weeks asking where "her" puppy was! She can't remember if she had breakfast, but she remembers the lap puppy from two weeks ago!

I decided to call the original foster mom, April, to see if there were any puppies still available from that litter. The mom and puppies were rescued from Bastrop, TX.

Me: Hi April! Say, I was just wondering if you still had any puppies from Nebula's litter?

April: There is only ONE left!

TO BE CONTINUED......

I am sure my experience with Alzheimer's is very similar to others in the same situation and in some ways maybe very different. Hopefully by sharing my experiences and adventures with my mom can help others that are new to the situation or disease. If I can raise awareness and a few smiles, I feel I have done a good thing writing this book. If you are a caregiver for someone with Alzheimer's, it's important to have breaks, take time for yourself. Patience is paramount even when they drive you crazy because they have asked you the same question 25 times in an hour! I wish everyone love and happiness in this crazy uncertain world we live in. Life is short, make it all count.

Facebook – www.facebook.com/adventureswithalzheimers

Please follow us on Instagram #adventureswithalzheimers
www.adventureswithalzheimers.com

Please check out my friends Instagram - #doggiesfordementia

Made in the USA
Middletown, DE
29 June 2019